For God and Country

Fisher DeBerry with Bob Schaller, For God and Country

ISBN 1-929478-21-6

Cross Training Publishing
317 West Second Street
Grand Island, NE 68801
(308) 384-5762

Library of Congress Cataloging in Publication Data in Progress.

Published by Cross Training Publishing,
317 West Second Street
Grand Island, NE 68801

DEDICATION

I wish to dedicate the remarks in this book to the memory of my loving mother and grandparents in appreciation for the foundations for life that they gave me. To my wife Lu Ann, daughter Michelle, and son Joe, I love you so much and want to say thanks for understanding and allowing me to pursue my dream. To my fellow and former coaches and players at all levels, you have taught me so much and have given me more than you will ever know. I appreciate your commitment to me personally and to the schools and programs that we have been privileged to serve. Nobody does anything by himself, and if it weren't for the wonderful secretaries and the administrative and support people, there would be no football team to coach. I hope for those who take the time to read this book by one of the best writers I know, Bob Schaller, that you will be challenged to serve God and our great nation and to become more compassionate and serve people.

INTRODUCTION

When Fisher DeBerry was asked about doing this book, his first response was, "Me? Really? Why?"

He is a humble man, yet his unique humor—and sometimes vocabulary—make his story that much more colorful and inspirational, all in the same sentence at times.

Taking a short biographical route and then weaving in Coach DeBerry's lessons for life, *For God and Country* allows Coach a chance to explain where he's come from and how much those experiences—and people—have shaped him into the man he is today.

His unique ability to quote the Bible to motivate, gain perspective or simply find sustenance, makes him a man different from most in college athletics. He lists his foundations, all of which revolve around faith.

Coach DeBerry was very firm when he said he didn't want this book "to glorify me in any way." However, it was impossible to get a full picture of this charming yet complex man without having those who have influenced him, and those he has influenced, talk about him.

To that end, several chapters conclude with "FISH(er) Stories," authored by former players and coaches—as well as others—who have been a big part of Coach DeBerry's life. Some are humorous. Some are heartfelt. Others deal with lessons learned from the coach, while some talk about the profound influence his faith and insights had, and continue to have, on their own lives.

The players and coaches who were generous enough to write about their experiences with Coach DeBerry, unfailingly ended our conversations with their offering of thanks for being included, when the reality was that they were the ones who were giving of their time. Even Chad Hennings, who wrote the foreword, took time out of mini-camp for the Dallas Cowboys to put his words on paper. That's as much a testimony to the special qualities of Coach DeBerry as it is to the men he coached, or coached with, who were so willing to offer their thoughts on Coach DeBerry for this project.

Thanks to Kathy Shipley and Chris Zelsnack of the Air Force Academy football office and Troy Garnhardt of the Academy's Sports Information Department for keeping this project on track. And a special thanks to Lu Ann DeBerry, the coach's wife, for her time, insights and sense of humor.

–Bob Schaller

FOREWORD BY
CHAD HENNINGS, DALLAS COWBOYS

When I think about Fisher DeBerry, the thing that strikes me first is the tremendous influence he's had on so many young men.

He always has stressed that we maintain a balance in our lives to our faith, family, commitment to the community and our jobs. All of those issues are very instrumental in molding young people, especially those who come to the United States Air Force Academy to serve their country.

When I first came to the Air Force Academy as a fourth-classman, I didn't weigh much more than 200 pounds. I knew I would play football at some point, but I thought it would be as a tight end because that's where my interest and the majority of my expertise were in high school.

Actually, during my first summer at the Academy, I just wanted to make it through Basic Cadet Training and my fourth-class year.

As it turned out, I was switched to the defensive line during the spring of my fourth-class year. Unfortunately, I sprained my ankle, so I wasn't able to perform to the best of my ability in front of the coaches. Add on to that the fact that I hadn't played much defense and didn't know as much on that side of the ball.

But I kept in mind what Coach DeBerry had told us about taking care of our priorities first, and then everything else will take care of itself. That's what happened for me. I put in the time academically and militarily and worked very hard in the weight room during the off-season.

Coach DeBerry believed in me the whole time. From there I went on to become a starter, win the Outland Trophy and eventually land where I am now, with the Dallas Cowboys.

I still reflect on my time with Coach DeBerry often—and fondly. Since I graduated, I have an even deeper appreciation of how he looked out for us. When a player would encounter a difficulty academically or militarily, Coach DeBerry would care about the person first instead of worrying about the football end of it. That is, if a player had to get some things in order, Coach DeBerry wasn't like some coaches who might take the attitude, "Let's do what gets you back on the field the quickest." That's what sets Coach DeBerry apart.

He is a football coach, however, first he is a Christian, a father and a husband—and football coach comes after all of that. He's a great role model for all of us in that he shows us how to be professional at our jobs, but that the first thing is caring for others. He always preaches to "take care of your brother" from the day his players show up.

That's Coach's forte—developing the sense of accountability that young people need today. He always pushed the team approach—he is constantly striving for that. The young men who come into the Academy and play football are often borderline Division I-A players. However, the way Coach DeBerry and his staff get that group to play together so well is where the success comes in. He makes it all fit together.

That's his system—in life and in football. Watch out for your brother; don't leave a stone unturned on your own responsibilities. It would be very hard to put another head coach in there and see him have the kind of success Coach DeBerry has had. It really takes a unique individual to succeed as a coach at the Air Force Academy.

Coach always motivates the players to believe in themselves and in the system. He can show them that if they work hard and always work for the team, they will have success.

I flew the A-10 "Warthog," a close air support aircraft, after graduating from the Academy. When the Air Force went through a reduction-in-force after the Gulf War, it wanted military members to leave the service. The Air Force waived my pilot training commitment, but I still had one year remaining on my Academy commitment before I could join the NFL. So, I called Coach DeBerry.

"Can I come back there and be a coach for a year?" I asked him over the phone.

"No problem," Coach said. "We'd love to have you back."

Not long thereafter, the military waived the service academy commitment, which would allow me to join the NFL and the Dallas Cowboys right away. However, I had made a commitment to Coach DeBerry. With the way I was raised by my family and the influence Coach DeBerry had on me, I still planned to honor my commitment to go back and coach at the Academy for the following year.

"Coach," I said, "I gave you my word that I would come back. I will if that's what's best for the Academy and the football program."

"No, Chad," Coach said. "You will do more for the Air Force and for Falcon football by playing in the NFL than coming back here and coaching."

So, I pursued my dream of playing in the NFL. It's ironic because we all have the option of leaving the Academy after our third-class year (sophomore year at civilian universities) with no obligation to the Air Force. A lot of guys who develop late are hitting their peak at that time. They have made themselves into Division I-A players and could easily transfer after that second year.

That hardly ever happens though, and the reason is that Coach DeBerry and his coaching staff are father figures to a lot of the guys. He makes that commitment to you, so you make it to him. The commitment he has to his players, his staff and the program, leads us all to appreciate and respect what a commitment is all about.

CONTENTS

1

Small Town, Big Hearts

When I was 3 years old, I was drugged.

That's right, I was drug by my grandmama to church every time the church doors opened, whether it was Wednesday night or Sunday morning for Sunday school and church.

My upbringing really impacted me, teaching me life lessons and getting a start down the proper avenue on this highway of life.

I was born in Cheraw, South Carolina, on June 9, 1938. My mother and father separated before my first birthday. My father was in the military, so I never did see much of him. Therefore, there wasn't enough between us for the formative bond between father and son.

I never really knew my dad. he left my mother when I was a year old, and five years later, they divorced. I didn't see my father very often and I don't have a lot of memories about the brief times we did spent together. He developed a very serious alcohol problem and died when I was 12 years old.

Since my father wasn't around, my mother had to make some difficult decisions, as did my grandparents—my mother's parents. When I was 2 years old, I don't know that my mother even had a nickel to her name—literally.

My mother had nowhere to go, so my grandparents took us in. To me that was the ultimate example of love and sacrifice for a family. My mother worked very hard and never made more than minimum wage. She often had two jobs, working as a seamstress and at a drycleaning store. I really learned to appreciate my mother's work ethic. She never complained about going to work. She knew she had a responsibility to me, and that also showed me what commitment was all about.

Since my mother was working, I spent a lot of time being raised by my grandmother. In fact, I called my grandma "Mother" and my mother "Mimi."

My grandfather was always there for me as well. He worked 42 years for the Atlantic Coastline railroad. He also taught me about a great work ethic. He didn't make a lot of money, but he did what he had to do to make ends meet for our family.

Every Saturday, we'd go downtown in Cheraw to pay bills he owed to various businesses, and to pay a portion to everybody else he owed, to keep his good name. We'd end our Saturday walks with a trip to the fish market because we'd have fish every Saturday—that was a big deal in our home. He'd let me choose the fish, and I was so proud to have that responsibility.

We'd have chicken on Sunday. We'd go out to where we kept our chickens and he'd let me pick out the chicken we were going to eat that Sunday. I'd chase that chicken around until I got it. Then we'd hem him up; grandpa would wring his neck and we'd take him inside. We'd put the chicken in water and clean him, getting all the feathers off him.

My grandpa really loved his family and worked hard to provide for us. He'd garden in the morning and just work himself into a frenzy doing that. Then at three in the afternoon, he'd head off to work at the railroad until midnight.

We were blessed to have three meals a day. Sometimes it

was milk and hotcakes at night, but it was food. Grandmother prided herself on cooking. She was always there. She always knew where I was. I might not have been in the yard, but I was playing ball across the street at the high school field.

No, we didn't have the perfect family life because I didn't have a father there. But I learned from a very loving family how to behave, and I learned what was important in life. Nothing was more important in that home than church and family. I learned about Christian principles and faith, especially from my grandmother.

My grandmother had such a caring attitude and great work ethic. When I was older, I didn't get to drive the car if I missed church. So on many a Sunday I'd be the only boy in the choir at church, but I'm glad my grandmother brought me up that way. I'm not saying I saw it that way all the time when I was growing up!

Probably the person who had the most influence on me was my grandmother. She gave me the foundation of my faith. She taught me about loyalty and commitment. She certainly was committed to me and everything I tried to do. She always quoted Scripture to me as situations arose in my life.

My mother was so loyal to our family. She was a very beautiful woman and was very stylish, taking pride in the way she looked. Certainly, she didn't have a lot of money to spend on fancy clothes, hairstyles or makeup. But she made the best of what she did have and she always looked very pretty. She passed up several opportunities to get married so she could stay with us.

Our house sat right across the street from the high school football field, which doubled as the baseball field in the spring and summer. I'd leave home early in the morning to start playing sports or just to watch the big kids.

I had a lot of friends who were into sports. Whatever the

season was, we played sports. I think it kept me out of trouble more than anything.

As kids we'd play tackle football on Saturdays early in the morning until noon. Nobody had more fun than we did.

Every Saturday my mother would give me a quarter for the matinee picture show, so I could watch from noon until three. Back then, you could go to the movies for nine pennies. Popcorn cost you a dime. Soda pop cost six pennies. That's how you'd spend your quarter. The movie would get over, and we'd all race back to the field to play football. In the spring and summer, we played baseball.

My mother saved up her money and bought me a very expensive set of music books. It was like a collection of music encyclopedias. I was taking piano lessons because she wanted me to be well rounded and expose me to as many cultural things as possible to, I guess, widen my horizons.

When I was in the fifth grade, I was the batboy for the high school baseball team. At the same time, my mother was trying to give me music lessons. The baseball team was playing in the state championship game the same night I had a piano recital. It was at the elementary school in town, one of those things where the piano teacher's students all performed to kind of show what they learned and how much progress they had made. Well, the baseball field was just next door to that elementary school. I felt bad because I wanted to be at the game.

I was sitting at the piano wearing my best Sunday clothes, but my heart was with the baseball team which was playing for the state championship. Because I had been with them all year, I couldn't think about the recital. I forgot my recital piece and I hit about two chords and just drew a blank. I sat there for a second, hit another note and then realized my heart wasn't into it. I ran off the stage, threw my bow tie up in the air and ran to the ballpark—thus bringing an abrupt end to my musical career.

On the field that night, we won the state championship and I shagged bats in my Sunday clothes. I think my mother understood. I know I embarrassed my mother on that night, and I felt very badly about that. She made such a sacrifice to get me those lessons.

Certainly, there's irony in this story because today there's nothing I love more than sitting down and listening to piano on CD. I do it for hours and hours—nothing relaxes me more than that. Maybe some day I'll come back to it and learn how to play the piano. I'm still not Fisher Von Beethoven—I don't know that I could tell you where a middle-C is. But I do have passion for the music. Even though I didn't learn it the way I was supposed to, I believe my appreciation and respect for music was born out of my mother's decision to sign me up for piano.

I was very fortunate to start working in the locally owned grocery store, McBride's Market, when I was only in fifth grade. At first, I worked on the weekend unloading trucks. I bagged groceries and stocked shelves. This was the kind of blue-collar work that I think kids really can learn a lot from. I'd get a good workout lifting the boxes. It would tire me out, even later when I was in high school, so I'd get right home because I realized the importance of a good night's sleep. More importantly it taught me the practical lessons of responsibility and accountability. I had to be at work at a certain time. I had to take pride in my appearance and had to meet certain requirements in terms of how I did my job and how much work I got done each day.

I worked up to bagging groceries, which was fun because I got to deal with the public. Then I worked all the way up to the meat market. I was so blessed to have the McBride family take such an interest in me. I took what little money I made and did just like my granddaddy did: I'd go around town on Saturday mornings while in high school and pay everyone I owed part of my bill. I had bought a lot of clothes on credit in town—credit was your good name back then—so I wanted to keep that good name.

I'd come home from college in the summer and pick right up working at McBride's, and even some at the men's clothing store and at a drygood's store, Belk's Department Store (where I had worked starting in junior high school).

We'd sell snow cones or chili out front depending on whether it was summer or winter. I was learning about getting my hands dirty and sweating a little to make a buck. And I was keeping busy, so even if I had the opportunity to get in trouble, I couldn't have—I always had something to do. That's kind of another benefit of living in a small town: If you were doing something wrong, someone would find out about it. In a small town, nobody is good at keeping secrets. So eventually, what you did was going to come back to you through your parents. If you were getting in trouble, that meant you were wrecking the good name your family had worked on for decades. That was an important lesson in accountability.

Another lesson came along at that time, and unfortunately, I chose to learn it the hard way. My friends and I were downtown on a weekend. One of the guys in our group threw a Coke bottle through a glass sign at a flower and gift shop. We, of course, scattered, and took off after the act. When I headed home not an hour later, my grandfather was waiting for me. He already had been called about what happened and was told that I had been seen in the group. He took me outside and wore out my backside a bit. He didn't want me doing things like that. It was wrong that I was in that group and wrong that we hurt those hard working folks' business—the guys and I had to pay to replace the sign. Another important lesson was that I wasn't just wrecking my name if I continued down that road; I'd be tarnishing my family's good name, one that they had worked so hard to build.

When I was in high school, my granddaddy developed tuberculosis. Modern medicine was still decades away, so he had to go live in what was called a "TB Sanatorium." That put a big strain on my grandmother and mother.

My mother took over all the shopping and other responsibilities because my grandmother didn't drive. That was a big change for our family. I saw how devoted my mother was to my grandmother. She knew how devoted my grandmother and grandfather had been to her and me, so she knew it was her calling to do the same.

My mother turned down another marriage proposal to see me through high school and college. Had she not turned that down, I don't know that I would've gone to college. Her constant encouragement and the fact that she and my grandmother were always there preaching the importance of education, was the difference in me pursuing my education. There weren't many in my high school class of '52 who went to college. My grandmother also insisted that I go to college because I was just like my mother in the respect that I felt like when I graduated from high school, I should stick around and provide for my mother and grandmother, as they had always done for me.

Our senior year, the football team wasn't going to be very good—though we had been in the state playoffs the past few years. Unfortunately, we only had a few starters returning.

On the Wednesday before our first conference game, I went home after practice and saw that I had a big knot in my thigh. I didn't know what it was. Since I was the quarterback,

I assumed it had just come from a lick, and it was a Charlie Horse or something. It got so bad that evening, though, I couldn't move. I walked a few blocks to a restaurant in town where I knew the coaches would be having dinner.

They took me to a doctor right away. From that evening to an hour before game time on Friday, I had 13 treatments from the doctor at his office. After each treatment, though, I ran home five blocks, which just irritated it all over again. I was just young and naïve, I guess. I ended up having a decent season, but we just weren't very good that year. A lot of teams really knocked me around that year because we had beaten them pretty badly the past few years. I had played on a Legion baseball team that had done really well. When we played them in football, they really went after me in friendly competition.

It was a tough year because as one of the few remaining players from that period, the other teams really had it in for me. I learned a lot, though, and met some good folks.

We had a senior trip scheduled to Washington, D.C., but since several of us were on the baseball team and played the night we left, the whole senior class had to wait for us to go. We ended up going with Belton Laney and his wife, Frances, who were the chaperones for the trip, as well as the group leaders in our church. Mr. Laney took me to watch the Boston Red Sox play the Washington Senators while we were on the trip. I got to meet Ted Williams and all the stars from that era because a friend from Cheraw, Tom Brewer, pitched for the Red Sox. In fact, when Tom was home in Cheraw before going to spring training each year, I'd play catcher for him so he could keep his arm in shape, which was a real thrill for me.

At the end of my senior year of high school, I played summer league baseball as always. But I played for a team in Darlington, which was 30 miles away from Cheraw. I'd travel back and forth each week. I'd hitch-hike down and then a coach or friend would bring me home. During that final year before college, I'd go down to Darlington on Monday and stay all week, and then a relative or someone would come to get me on the weekend and bring me home.

I wasn't the best example of a student all the time in school. In high school, we were mischievous. One time, my friends and I turned a chicken loose in study hall, the day after Halloween. It was flying wildly around the room, doing it's business all over the place. Some guy rang its neck and threw it out in the trash pile.

That afternoon, we were getting ready for football practice. I was sitting on the bleachers getting taped by the coach in plain view of that trash pile. The mayor's house was right next to the field. His little boy, "Pokey," came over to watch practice every day, and this day was no exception. The 6-year-old was carrying this big bag of candy from trick-or-treating the night before.

Well, Pokey saw the rooster lying on the pile. He turned his candy bag upside down, dumping the candy all over the ground. He opened the bag and stuffed that chicken in there. He came over to Coach and me, with his face all lit up. "My goodness, look at what I found!" he proudly proclaimed. "And it's mine, all mine!"

Coach looked at me, his face pale. I just smiled.

"It sure is, Pokey," I said smiling.

You have to understand; we were in a rural area and just raised under a different pretense and era that exists today. Back then, it was harmless fun, but I reckon today we'd have drawn out animal rights protesters and everyone else.

Living in Cheraw, there wasn't much to do. I often tell audiences that I didn't walk until I was three because there was no where to go! After all, we had just one traffic light. Down the state highway, 30 miles to the south, was Pageland—the watermelon capital of the state and the entire South. In fact, one year Lu Ann was a queen in the Watermelon Festival down there. Anyway, truckers would come through downtown hauling watermelons to the northeast. If that light was red and they stopped for it, we'd sneak into the back of those trucks and grab us a watermelon or two.

In the classroom, I liked all the subjects, except for math. That became a challenge.

It started during my sophomore year of high school. I was a smart-alec. Girls and athletics were all that was important to me. I had a math teacher, Miss Frances Burch, who had a reputation as a demanding teacher. She told me, "You're the sorriest math student I've ever had."

I was on the border of failing her class. In fact, it came down to the last day of school as to whether I'd pass or not. I did pass, and I was so relieved I didn't feel a sense of accomplishment or anything meaningful. I hadn't applied myself and I had worked against the system, not with it. All I did was keep my head above water—I wasn't learning to swim in math, so to speak, I was just treading water.

During my junior year of high school, I didn't take math either semester, but I thought about Miss Burch a lot. I thought about how she had challenged me. I didn't like the way I responded to that challenge. The bad taste never left my mouth. When I would see her in the halls at school, I felt bad because I hadn't shown her that I had a good work ethic and that down deep I really was a good kid.

So my senior year of high school, I signed up for math. My counselor told me it would greatly enhance my chances of getting into college. So I took both geometry and algebra from Miss Burch. Those were arguably the toughest two classes in our entire school systems from one of the toughest—but one of the most talented and well revered—teachers in the region, maybe even the state.

I worked very hard and paid attention in class. I worked hard on my homework and asked good questions. I didn't cut corners this time and I didn't work just to pass. Indeed, I put in all the time I needed, which because of my lack of interest and maybe aptitude in math, was a lot of time. I picked up two A's that year in math. I believe I got more satisfaction from those classes than any others I ever took.

I was recruited a little bit coming out of high school for football and baseball. I verbally committed to the Citadel during my senior year of high school. As I thought about it and prayed on it after visiting the Citadel over Spring Break, I felt it wasn't the best place for me. After all, my high school coach called Wofford College in Spartanburg, South Carolina, a few hours northwest of Cheraw. The coaches at Wofford had seen me play in a high school all-star game, but since it was April, they already had given away all of their scholarship money.

I was able to get a little academic help and received my academic textbooks for playing baseball. My mother had saved some money from my dad's social security, so I packed to go to college.

Upon arriving at Wofford, I was greeted by the dean of students, Frank Logan. He told me, "You won't make it," and I took that as a challenge. Of course, he probably told all the other kids that, too, but I took it as a challenge and used it as motivation.

When I went off to college, my grandmother had told me, "You might be a little sheltered—a lot of situations you find yourself in, you won't have been in before, but if you ask yourself, 'What would Jesus do if he were in my shoes?' then you'll be just fine and will receive the right answer." I recommend this to my players and audiences today!

What a beautiful piece of advice from a very beautiful woman. I wholeheartedly endorse that philosophy and practice it. Most of the time, you will come out just fine. It's once again a case of just trying to do what's right. No, it might not appear that way to other people at times, but being in the majority is not the most important thing.

I went to church because it was a habit my family had developed in me. So I went every Sunday when I was in college. I went, not because I had to or needed it—though I did need it—but because that's how I was raised.

I really enjoyed that first year at Wofford, and playing baseball in college was a lot of fun. My second year at Wofford, I went out for football and that got me a little more help. Of course, back then it cost only $900 a year to go to school. I had a $300 scholarship for football, plus books through baseball. I had an academic work study as well that paid me for working in the dean's office, helping file papers and anything else that needed to be done.

On Friday nights, I'd go to watch Spartanburg High School's football team play, but I wasn't there as a fan. They played in our college stadium. I worked selling hot dogs until halftime, at which time I'd have to return to my room to make curfew since we'd have a football game the next day. But those few bucks each Friday night also helped me get by.

Of course, I had fun in college; but again, some of the pranks were pretty bad. Once we took a teammate's car and hid it behind the Sears Roebuck and Co. store there in Spartanburg. Turns out he called the police, so we all panicked and didn't say anything. They didn't find that car for three days.

At Wofford, I was still far too much of a prankster. I had

a philosophy class that had a blind professor. My friends and I would sit in the back of the room and answer roll call each day and then leave. We had to be there for role call because you could only miss so many classes without flunking or being dropped. By the end of class each day, the professor had only one or two students left. But that was enough—because one of them alerted the professor to what was going on. So, he somehow trained his seeing-eye dog to sit at the back of the class and growl at anyone who got up. The first couple of days, I thought I could beat his system. But he'd hear that dog start to growl and he'd yell, "Sit down, DeBerry."

We had a Spanish professor, Dr. Adams. Between our class time and the class before us, he'd go down to get coffee at the college cantina. There was a rule that if the professor was 10 minutes late to class, the students could leave. So we'd go up to the second floor and watch for him to come across the campus. We'd run downstairs and lock the front door. Then when he went around the building, we'd unlock the front door and slip out of the building because we had made him 12 or 15 minutes late. If he'd been able to come in the front door, he'd have never been late.

My junior year, I was enrolled in Reserve Officer Training Course at Wofford (ROTC). I don't know if I did it to serve the country as much as I did it for that $50 a month because that money really helped me make ends meet.

While I was in college, my mother sent me money—bless her heart—because she barely had enough money to make her own ends meet. But in the mail I'd get $5 a week or $10 to $15 a month from her—whatever she could send.

My grandfather died during my senior year of college, so I really wouldn't have continued my education in college were it not for my mother and grandmother. I remember talking to my grandma when I was thinking about leaving college and heading back to Cheraw.

"I'm gonna come home and help you guys," I told her.

"No," my grandmother insisted. "We've gotten along well all these years. We'll get along fine. The most important thing is for you to finish your education. I'll kick your behind if you come home."

My mother and grandmother were able to maintain that home that I grew up in. In fact, my mother lived in that same house until she grew old and went into the nursing home.

I liked everything academically in college, particularly the sciences and the humanities. I was especially fond of any class that dealt with people. Actually, I took pre-med up until my senior year in college. A lot of my buddies were going on to dental and medical school. But after three years, I lacked a class in organic chemistry because I chose instead to take a class that got me state certified as a teacher. So I ended up majoring in educational psychology and teaching. I also completed my final year of eligibility as well.

After I graduated in 1960, I had a seven-month stint coaching varsity football, junior varsity basketball and baseball, and teaching science at Bennettsville (South Carolina) High School, which had been our arch rivals. People in Cheraw couldn't understand this.

I was commissioned in the United States Army as an officer and went on active duty in 1961.

I did two years of active duty. Basic training had been at Fort Benning, Georgia, before my junior year of college. Boot camp was competitive, like football. You competed with and against your classmates, and there was nowhere else that demanded such a sense of responsibility and accountability.

In fact, I recommend the military to any young person today. The discipline, time management and team building skills you learn will remain with you the rest of your life. Even if you join the Reserves or the National Guard, the military can help a young person find the focus and direction he or she needs in life, especially in this day and age.

I went to base school at Fort Ben Harrison in Indianapolis, Indiana, where the military trained me in personnel and recruiting. Then it was on to Pennsylvania to the U.S. Army Recruiting Mainstation where I was a personnel psychologist. The University of Pittsburgh was nearby and I was able to get most of the work for my master's degree out of the way. I did my graduate work in guidance and counseling because I thought that was important.

I thought about staying in the service when my two years were up. During the Berlin crisis, the Army had taken away all of our Majors and Colonels and I received some good command experience on active duty. So, I had a good chance to keep climbing the chain, had I stayed in. It looked like my next assignment would have been at the special services office in Munich, Germany, and that really appealed to me. However, I had received a lot of calls from my coaches and administrators to return to high school coaching, which had a big influence on me. I chose to return to civilian life, though I remained in the active reserves for three years.

I also did duty as the commander of a ready reserves unit in Florence, South Carolina, reaching the rank of captain. That time in the military just reinforced my love for this country. I get goose bumps when I hear "Stars and Stripes Forever," or the National Anthem before a game. One of my favorite songs ever is Lee Greenwood's "God Bless the USA."

When I left active duty 1963, I went back to Florence to become an assistant football coach, head baseball coach and teacher. I was a guidance counselor and taught biology and science.

I also was able to finish up my master's degree at the University of South Carolina during the summer. I really wanted that Master's because my grandmother encouraged me to get it. It meant so much to her and my mother.

So I was ready to head down the road of life. I didn't know that around the next corner was a woman who would change my life forever—and complete my life as well.

2

The Ultimate Kind of Heart

My wife, Lu Ann, is such a big part of who I am that I can't express it in words. It's a feeling like no other. All of the success we've had as parents and in coaching has been done together. I don't pretend to take credit for the lion's share of how our kids turned out. She was the one who put so much of her life into being a great mother.

Growing up, I had known Lu Ann's family for a long time. They were members of our church. Her mother worked at the bank opening new accounts and greeting all of the customers. Her mother was a very stylish, beautiful woman and very pleasant. Lu Ann's father worked in the drycleaners before going into the furniture business with a good friend.

Her parents were very well respected in the community. I always thought Lu Ann was a pretty girl. She was a wonderful person and very respected in the community. It was well known that she had high moral standards. She also worked in the summer to help pay for her college, so she had the kind of work ethic, sense of responsibility, accountability and commitment that everyone admired.

It was during her senior year of college that I had just returned to South Carolina after getting out of the Army to teach and coach.

Lu Ann was a student at Winthrop College. Unbeknownst

to either of us, we were both in Cheraw at the same wedding one weekend. A teammate of mine was trying to get a date with a high school classmate of mine and wanted me to go along to help things go smoothly and help them get to know each other. I told him that I would go later, but I had made a commitment to go to a friend's wedding first.

So I went to the wedding. I walked into the reception and stopped atop the stairs leading to the main room. I looked down the steps and saw a young woman talking to someone who appeared to be her mother. I looked at the young woman in the low-cut pink dress and I thought, "Wow, who is that?"

I ended up recognizing them and went up to talk to Lu Ann. I asked her if she'd like to go to a pool party later that night.

"Well, I think that I might," she said.

We went to the pool party, but it didn't go as well as I thought it would because my friend wasn't conducting himself in a very good way. I was worried that Lu Ann would have a bad impression of me because of the bad behavior my friend was exhibiting—I wasn't too happy about it, and I told him so.

I asked Lu Ann if she'd go out with me the next night. We went to a drive-in movie with three other couples and saw Elvis Presley in "Bye-Bye Birdie." Being in a group, we still didn't have much of a chance to talk, so I asked her out again. We ended up dating that summer, and I really enjoyed her company.

The summer ended. Lu Ann started her student-teaching in Greer, South Carolina, and I went off three hours away to Florence to coach and teach.

I really missed her. I'd go see her and take her out. It was neat because she lived with a wonderful, elderly woman named Mrs. Mayfield. She was a witty and charming

75-year-old who had a very big influence on our lives. We'd sit out on the porch and talk to her for hours and hours.

Whenever I'd go over there to pick up Lu Ann for a movie or dinner, Mrs. Mayfield would tell us as we walked out the door, "Remember who you are," something she probably told her own children years and years earlier.

That saying means, don't embarrass yourself or do anything that your family would regret. Remember how you were raised and that you know right from wrong. In fact, it's something we said to our kids decades later when they'd go out at night. I still tell my players that on Saturdays after our games. It really made quite an impression on us.

So Lu Ann and I dated and enjoyed our time together. I went the longest time without telling her that I loved her because I wanted to say it only if I was sure. I didn't know what that kind of love meant or entailed before Lu Ann, but soon I did. I'd miss her so much.

"Man," I thought to myself, "it's so tough not being around her."

In the fall of 1964, I knew I couldn't be away from her much longer. As Christmas approached, I went to her father's store and bought her a TV that I gave her for Christmas.

"Well," her father said, "you're giving her a TV for Christmas? There must be something there."

So I went by early the next year and saw her parents. I asked them what they thought about me and if they thought I'd be suitable to marry their wonderful daughter. They gave me their blessing.

Someone else in their family wasn't as convinced. The aunt of Lu Ann's mother lived just around the corner from my family when I was growing up. She told Lu Ann's parents a story about how when I was little I laid down on the sidewalk and wouldn't let her by.

"You're not going to let Lu Ann marry that naughty DeBerry boy are you?" the aunt asked Lu Ann's mother.

Well, blocked sidewalk or not, Lu Ann's parents deemed me suitable. I was very happy.

While I was on active duty in the Army in Pennsylvania, the man I rented from owned a jewelry story. He had told me, "When you decide to get married, I want you to give me the honor of selling you the ring," so I did. The ring finally came in, and after I got done officiating a high school basketball game in March of 1965, I proposed to her in my grandmother's backyard and gave her the ring.

We were married on June 26, 1965. We went to Williamsburg, Virginia for our honeymoon. Ten years later, we went back to the same place to celebrate our anniversary.

Soon after we were married, we moved to Florence and rented a very small house. I coached at McClenaghan High School where we made many good friends. Those were the happiest years imaginable. We weren't making much money and had almost nothing in the bank. While trying to serve the community, we were teaching and enjoying our students and players—best of all, we had each other!

Five years later, one of my mentors, Coach Jim Brakefield, who coached me in baseball and football at Wofford, had been elevated to head football coach at Wofford. Coach Brakefield offered me a chance to join his coaching staff at Wofford. I also had a chance to go to a big high school for more money with Coach Dick Sheridan (later the coach at North Carolina State). But I wanted to find out what college coaching was all about. Lu Ann and I prayed a lot about the decision.

She knew that I was honored to be asked to come back and coach at my alma mater. It was like coming home again.

I had to take a $3,000 pay cut, and we weren't too

excited about that. I worked in the summers at a sporting goods store and an auto parts store to help us make ends meet. We had even less money than before, but we were even happier together. I remember seeing the balance from our bank account at 98 cents a couple of times and thinking, "Great! We made it again."

I don't think you realize what true love is until you've been married five years or so, had your first child, and you've been through some adversity. We really were in love, as it turned out.

We knew when we got married we would give part of our salary to the church. My first salary was $3,600, so there wasn't a lot of money. But we knew it wasn't our money anyway; it was God's. So we gave him back ten percent first. Sure, there were a few days when we had 28 cents in the bank at the end of the month, but God has been faithful to us, and we've been faithful to the commitment we made to God. Yes, there were some lean times. We didn't miss a lot of meals, but there were times when all we had was some milk in the refrigerator, some bread on the table and some sugar maybe in the cabinet.

Our first child, Michelle, was born in 1967 and Joe was born in 1970. Becoming a father taught me so much about myself that I didn't know before. It also taught me patience. After Michelle was born, we decided our children were more important than work so Lu Ann stayed home. I joke that Lu Ann "didn't work another day in her life after Michelle was born." Of course, she slaps me upside the head when I say that because we both know she worked far harder—at a much more meaningful vocation as a mother—than I ever did.

I'd sit and watch her holding Michelle and realize that Lu Ann had all the foundations that I admired and respected in a woman—or any person, for that matter. She possessed not just the incredible physical beauty that she had and has, but inside her heart was the most beautiful thing on God's green Earth. As you spend more time together and the years passed, you have nothing if you don't have a good heart. She's everything I was ever looking for.

There are times when she and I wished we had more time together. The job has taken precedent at times. My life is about the "Three F's,"—Faith, Family and Football. That's the order of the way it should be. Occasionally, I get those out of order, and that's when I screw things up. However, Lu Ann has always been so supportive.

The materialistic things never overwhelmed her. Certainly, we've "done better" over the years, but that beautiful heart always has stayed strong and loving, and delivered a perspective and compassion that means the world to me and our relationship. She's so stable, steady and strong. Every decision we've made has been from our partnership. The first of those decisions was the move to Wofford in 1968.

The time at Wofford was important in so many ways. On the field, we lost our first two games and then won 21 straight games over the rest of that season and the next season. We had a good run at Wofford in those two years. We were ranked No. 1 in the NAIA poll and played Texas A&I for the national small college championship in 1969.

It was an incredible time of growth as a Christian, husband, coach and father. We had a very small staff, so we had to coach on both sides of the ball. Even though I spent most of my time coaching defense with Coach Gene Alexander, I did some work with the offense as well. It was a full-time staff of only four, so we shared a lot of ideas back and forth on both sides of the ball.

Coach Brakefield was hired by Appalachian State in 1970,

and he asked me to come with him as his top assistant coach. That meant a lot because I could tell he respected my abilities. I was the defensive coordinator and Buddy Sasser was the offensive coordinator. After five years, Buddy went to Wofford to become the head coach in 1974.

Jokingly, I said to Coach Brakefield, "Let me move to the offense." He smiled and didn't say anything. Since our defense was ranked sixth nationally in pass defense in 1974, I figured he'd probably keep me on defense. However, a few days later he said, "If that's what you want to do, we can do it."

My thinking was that it would be good experience for me to have some time on the offensive side of the ball, if I were ever to become a head coach. After all, I did know the offense and had a hand in helping develop it.

We made it work really quickly at Appalachian State, taking the program from the NAIA to the NCAA Division I-AA level. We had a winning season our first year. We got some players who fit into our system and some quarterbacks who were very good at executing the option.

The more you understand both sides of the ball, the better coach you are going to be. Certainly, there are some great college coaches today who spend a majority of their time on one side of the ball, and there are some head coaches who completely turn the offense and defense to their assistants. I think you gain a perspective and an idea of what your opponent is thinking if you've had experience on both sides of the ball.

That goes to show you that in most organizations you don't just walk in and run the place. You must talk to kids in recruiting, so you will have to put in time and work wherever you go. Football is just like a corporation. They won't make you the president or CEO the first day. Some of the best coaches are the ones who started on the scout team. Like in business, you start in one department. You can work from department to department—and back again to higher positions—within the same organization. The kind of employee who had that breadth of experience has a good idea of what it takes for the company to be successful. There are very few people who have started at the very top; most start at or near the bottom and work their way up.

When I coached in high school, I had to mark the fields up, tape ankles, issue equipment, manage a budget and drive the bus. I've been there, done that, as they say. I believe it's given me a good appreciation for everyone's job, a respect for what needs to be done and a good perspective that includes the whole picture.

So taking on offensive coordinator was really a good move for me. We really had a good run at Appalachian State. In 1975, '78 and '79, we ranked in the top 10 nationally in rushing, total offense or scoring while I was the offensive coordinator.

While I was at Appalachian State, I never stopped my fellowship with other Christians, including coaches. I'll admit that I never thought that I'd end up in the West. During that time at Appalachian, I had become good friends with a coach named Ken Hatfield. We met through the Fellowship of Christian Athletes summer camp and stayed in touch while he coached as an assistant at Tennessee and Florida. We'd talk on the phone and exchange thoughts and film.

The summer before Coach Brakefield decided to step down (he did after the 1979 season), I wasn't sure if I wanted to continue in coaching. There were certain things about a career in coaching that I wasn't sure I wanted to do for the next 30 years, so I had to evaluate where I was and where I was heading.

I wanted to give teaching a real chance, which would

broaden my perspective and give context to both careers—teaching and coaching.

I returned to teaching at Appalachian State after Coach Brakefield retired and even though I was offered to, I didn't stay on with the new coaching staff.

On the other hand, that was a tough period of time because we had just experienced so much success at Appalachian State. But I needed a break from coaching. At that point, I really needed to find out how I liked life as a full-time teacher or administrator at the college level.

Getting back in the classroom was a really positive thing for me because my love is for teaching.

Part of the job description as coaches is that we need to be teachers first and foremost. That time in the classroom also reminded me how much I like interacting with young people. Being around them in a classroom setting helped keep me abreast of what they were thinking and what the important issues and trends were in their lives. It really made me feel young again.

I might yet go back and take more classes. When I retire from coaching here, I still might try to become an elementary school principal, but I might be too old. I'm not sure school boards will hire a 65- or 70-year-old principal. Still, I think that's the best—and one of the most important—jobs in America. It's just always been a dream of mine to be an elementary school principal.

That spring at Appalachian State, I also realized that it was important to be constantly learning—I took classes at Appalachian State in the spring semesters while I was coaching there because my grandmother had instilled in me the importance of continuing your education.

I've never sent out a resume or sought out a job since I applied for my first high school job. Your day-to-day work, your values and the images you project should be enough to sell yourself. You shouldn't have to write some great essay about yourself, selling yourself. I guess I'd just have a hard time recommending myself for a job.

As I went to the classroom full-time and stepped away from football, Lu Ann and I prayed about it and decided we'd just go wherever the Good Lord led us—or stay at Appalachian State and teach.

Coach Hatfield called and said he wanted to install the wishbone offense at the Air Force Academy in Colorado Springs. Since we had so much success with that offense at Appalachian State the previous four years, he asked Coach Brakefield and me to come to the Academy and walk him through our offense and its nuances. Jim and I flew out to Colorado and spent a few days going through everything with Coach Hatfield and his staff. He didn't have an opening on his staff, so it wasn't like I went there to apply for a job. I was just kind of a consultant, spending time with a great man and the great coaches on his staff.

For the final day, Coach Hatfield and Coach Brakefield spent some time together while the assistant coaches took me skiing in the Rocky Mountains. We had a good time and I admired the fellowship and camaraderie among the coaching staff.

I really admired the Academy and what it stands for. I headed home and thought a lot about Colorado. I hadn't even been close to the Mississippi River for any length of time, much less clear on the other side of it. But there was no doubt in my mind that something special was going on at the Air Force Academy. That time spent with Coach Hatfield and his assistants, stimulated my interest in coaching again. I realized the things that I missed about coaching, especially the dialogue among the coaches and the interaction with the players. But I returned to Appalachian State prepared to continue my career as a college educator or administrator.

Low and behold, three weeks later Coach Hatfield called me. An assistant coach of his had left, and he had an opening for quarterback coach. Lu Ann and I prayed and talked about it. We really loved South Carolina and North Carolina. All of our roots were there. We also knew that the environment in Colorado and at the Academy would be good for our children. Plus, Ken's values and philosophy were so synonymous with mine that I thought it would be a good match in that respect. So, early in 1980, we moved to Colorado Springs.

Jim Bowman, an assistant athletic director at the Academy, remembers when Athletic Director Colonel John Clune came out of a meeting with Coach Hatfield, during which Hatfield asked if he could hire me. Colonel Clune grudgingly gave his approval.

"Oh, great," Clune said to Bowman. "Hatfield's just hired some guy named…uh, Drew Barry or something, from Appalachian something or another. And they're going to install the Wishbone! Can you believe that—the Wishbone! I think I'll go work on my resume."

I could understand his thinking. Air Force had won four games only once, with four two-win seasons and a one three-win season since 1974. Prior to that, Ben Martin had a good run as head coach over a 20-year span in the late 1950s, '60s, and '70s. Bill Parcells, who would go on to take both the New York Giants and New England Patriots to the Super Bowl, had been the Academy's head coach in 1978, following Martin. However, Parcells left after one season in which the Falcons went 3-8. Then, in 1979, the year before Ken hired me, Air Force was 2-9.

It didn't get much better during my first year at the Academy as an assistant as we went 2-9 in 1980. As the offense started to take hold, though, and the players grasped the system, we improved to 4-7 in 1981, my first season as offensive coordinator.

The 1982 season was even better as we went 8-5, including a 30-17 victory over Notre Dame and a 36-28 win over Vanderbilt in the Hall of Fame Bowl.

In the next year, 1983, it really all came together. We went 10-2, beating Notre Dame at South Bend, Indiana, and beating Mississippi, 9-3, in the Independence Bowl. Coach Hatfield was a hot coaching commodity, and he was hired to go back to his alma mater, the University of Arkansas, as head coach. Coach Hatfield had told me from day one that there were only two jobs in the entire country he'd leave the Academy for, Arkansas and the University of Missouri.

The players here endorsed me strongly for the head coach opening at the Air Force Academy. Coach Hatfield wanted me to go with him and that was a great opportunity. But our players at the Academy had worked so hard. They had made such a sacrifice and bought into the wishbone. They had developed such a belief in themselves that it would not have been fair to the kids or good for the program for all of us to pull out at once. Becoming the head coach at the Academy was also a great opportunity for me.

We had a solid first year, going 8-4—including another win at Notre Dame—and beating Virginia Tech, 23-7, in the Independence Bowl. A 12-1 year followed, in which we beat Notre Dame, 21-15, and downed Texas, 24-16, in the Blue-Bonnet Bowl.

As head coach, we followed up 1985 with a 6-5 record in 1986 and a 9-4 mark in 1987. We were accomplishing a lot of our goals. Our first goal every year is to win the Commander-in-Chief's Trophy, which goes to the service academy that does the best against each other—Air Force, Army and Navy.

Our second goal is to win the conference championship. We also have as a goal to beat Notre Dame—when it is on our schedule—and to continue to go to bowl games.

In 1988, we had our first losing season, going 5-7. We lost two games by a field goal and two others by a touchdown or less. I really asked the guys on the team and the coaching staff to re-commit themselves after the season. However, very early into the off-season my phone rang.

The coaching job had opened up at the University of South Carolina. That was my home-state university, the pride and joy of the state in which I was raised. I knew a lot of people back there, and it would have brought us closer to where our families lived.

We thought about everything. Our children really loved living in Colorado Springs, were established in very good schools and had wonderful friends. Everyone at the Academy had been very supportive of me. I couldn't walk down a hallway or street without having someone say, "That's okay, coach, you'll get 'em next year." Everyone really believed in the staff and me.

The deciding factor to stay, though, was what had happened at the end of the season: I had gone to every player on our team and every coach on our staff and asked for a commitment from them, which they were making. I felt it wasn't fair to abandon my commitment as we readied for spring ball. Maybe they could have gotten a better coach had I left, I don't know.

I did know that I wasn't leaving the people who had shown so much belief in me, especially during our first real stretch of adversity while I was head coach.

We rebounded in 1989, going 8-4-1, though we lost in the Liberty Bowl to Mississippi, 42-29. In 1990, we were 7-5 and picked up one of the biggest wins of my career, a 23-11 victory over heavily favored Ohio State in the Liberty Bowl.

Everything came together in 1991 when we went 10-3, beating Mississippi State in the Liberty Bowl. We had just one losing season since and in 1998, we reached our highest level, going 12-1. We defeated Washington, 45-25, in the O'ahu Bowl. Our only blemish was an upset loss at Texas Christian, 35-34.

I have had several chances to leave—but I have never pursued anything. I've always been flattered when I get contacted about an opening. I'll be real honest: Sometimes I couldn't believe the amount of money that was being offered, but I never make a decision predicated on money. I always want to make the decision that is best for my family. I do listen to anyone who wants to talk to me because I think I have that obligation to my family and staff to keep our options open. However, I've simply never found anything better than the Academy in terms of meeting our values, needs and other criteria for a job and lifestyle.

It's been about so much more than football at the Academy. In fact, I don't remember game scores and records from year to year or a particular player's statistics—I had to have all of these looked up for this project—but I can tell you about the people and personalities from each year. That's what you remember, the people and the character. The numbers are merely a product of what took place after the team chemistry developed and the attitude of the team was shaped.

Here are just a few examples—I could write a book just about the fine young men who have played at the Academy. However, I am limited to how many I can list in this format.

Our quarterback in 1982 was a fine young man named Marty Louthan. He played several positions for us—the last being quarterback. He was just too good, as it turned out, not to play quarterback. I remember one time on the sideline during the game; I was really worked up. I was gabbing a mile a minute and racing around the sideline. Marty was real calm and cool. He got me to stop for a minute and looked me in the eye.

"Coach, if you'll just settle down and quit yelling, we'll get this thing straightened out," Marty said.

Since then, I've held my poise a little better. Marty did a lot for kids in the community. So did our quarterback from 1995-96, Beau Morgan. After games, rather than going to a party or out to eat with his teammates, Beau would go down to the Salvation Army or shelters and help out or, like a lot of players through the years, he'd go to be part of the mentoring and witness programs. We've had a lot of kids who did that, and I'm so proud of them.

We had a running back here named Anthony Roberson, who played at Sierra High School in Colorado Springs before coming to the Academy. On September 1, 1995, the day before the opening game of the season, my phone rang.

"Hi, coach," the voice said. "How are you?"

I could hear a lot of noise in the background.

"I'm fine," I answered.

"This is Anthony," the voice said. I recognized Anthony Roberson's voice.

"Coach, I just called to say good luck against BYU tomorrow," Anthony said.

Here he was, flying back from Bosnia in his F-16 after a mission, and he thought enough to call and wish us luck. What a special young man. We went on to beat BYU, 38-12.

Our quarterback in 1999 was Cale Bonds. He wasn't a prototypical quarterback or wishbone quarterback, but he worked at all the things he needed to do in order to become a great option quarterback. We had a 160-pound quarterback from 1987-89 named Dee Dowis. This young man was a magician on the field. He might have been small, but he had the heart of someone seven-feet-tall and 300 pounds—his heart was just so much bigger than his physique and his faith was impressive as well. We had another quarterback in 1989, Lance McDowell, who made a huge impression on me by the way he carried himself. He wasn't a starter, yet he was elected team captain. That says a lot about the example he set for the team.

So many of these young men touched my life—and I know I'm leaving hundreds of them out. If I've had an impact on any of them, I am grateful, and humbled, and I can tell you that they have deeply impacted me. I've learned from all of them.

"Not a great athlete, but ..."

Fisher DeBerry is just about the finest young man I've ever known.

Fisher played for me at Wofford College, first in baseball and then football. It was a small school, so coaches had to coach more than one sport. He was a good baseball player and worked hard in football. He had just a tremendous work ethic.

When he graduated, I was still an assistant coach. When I became the head coach at Wofford, the first thing I did was hire Fisher. When I became the head coach at Appalachian State, the first thing I did was call Fisher to bring him along. I'm 82 years old now, so I won't be coaching again. But if I did, the first call I'd make would be to Fisher. He always was such a hard worker, and that's the type of person you want in your program. He always was willing to do a little bit more to get the job done.

He was not a great athlete, as it were. He was all-state in high school, but he came from a small school. He was a small boy, too. But I always liked his enthusiasm. We'd have coaching clinics, and he'd get so excited that you'd have to about stop him. I'm so proud to hear that I've had a good effect on him. That's what you're in this business for, to help shape and encourage young people and to help them grow. Our job isn't necessarily to win. It is to make a young man a good man.

I've taken a lot of pride in seeing his success at the Air Force Academy. He's such a talented coach that he could coach any position and be so successful. When he came to me at Appalachian State, then as the defensive coach, and asked to be the offensive coordinator, I said yes. I knew he wanted a better knowledge of the whole picture. He had done such a tremendous job with the defense, and he did an amazing job with the offense after switching sides of the ball.

Jim Brakefield, former head coach, Wofford, Appalachian State

"Want to come out West?"

At the time, I didn't really want the job at the Air Force Academy when Bill Parcells left, but I ended up taking it. The Good Lord ended up putting the right people in my path.

God knew that Fisher DeBerry had a yearning for young people. Of course, coaching at a military academy is different. You have to see how the mission of the academies ties in to football. So you need coaches who see more than wins and losses.

I met Fisher through a Fellowship of Christian Athletes camp. I was at the University of Florida at the time coaching defensive backs. We played Alabama each year, which ran the option. So, I talked to Fisher and learned more about how to defend the Wishbone.

When I took over as head coach at the Air Force Academy, I knew we had to go to a different offense if we were ever going to be successful. With the kind of players we had, we had to run an offense that was all about execution and discipline: the Wishbone. I called Fisher, who was out of coaching at the time and had him and Coach Jim Brakefield come out to the Academy to break down the Wishbone for us. We went through film and everything. My assistant coaches took Fisher skiing the final day, while Coach Brakefield and me stayed behind. They all really liked Fisher, as did I. We didn't have an opening on our staff at the time.

Three weeks after Fisher and Coach Brakefield left, we

had an offensive assistant leave the Academy. We had some young quarterbacks coming in, and we knew Fisher would be good coaching them.

I went in to see Colonel John Clune, the distinguished athletic director, about hiring Fisher and putting in the Wishbone.

"Are you sure you're going to run this wishbone thing?" Colonel Clune asked me.

"John, you think a wishbone is something that comes out of a chicken," I answered. "We need to win, and this is our best chance."

I knew Colonel Clune was catching the dickens from alums, but he had a lot of faith. Colonel Clune is the architect for Air Force Academy athletics. He fought the hard battles through the years. He knew getting Air Force into the Western Athletic Conference was the right decision. We had a great superintendent out there as well, General Kenneth Tallman—boy, he was as strong as they come. Colonel Clune educated him on what was happening and how we could be competitive, including recruiting. In his one year as head coach, Bill Parcells did a good job of getting the overall program heading in the right direction by letting those in charge know what was needed in terms of resources, scheduling, equipment and coaching salaries. When Bill left the Academy, he went to the NFL with New England, but stayed only two months and came back to Colorado Springs. He stayed for a year and sold real estate. His wife, Judy, saw how miserable Bill was out of coaching, so he went back to the NFL, this time with the New York Giants. Of course, we all know how well that turned out.

So, we hired Fisher as quarterbacks coach, and he was the key to putting in the offense. Fisher and Lu Ann came out here and fit in right away. Fisher knew the offense and was just so full of enthusiasm. Because of his own background in the U.S. Army, he also believed in the system and the mission of the Academy.

He also knew that on the field we weren't going to beat anyone up and we weren't going to win right away. He knew we were operating in the lower echelon of college football and that we were building. So no one really knew if we'd be successful. Through hard work and patience, it worked out.

Fisher knows the difficulties of coaching at a military academy. The attrition rate approaches 40 percent some years. But he sees the upside of it. People thought Air Force football would never be a consistently winning program, including a lot of people on the inside. However, we got it started, and the run Fisher has had since then speaks for itself.

Ken Hatfield, head coach, Rice, former head coach Air Force, Arkansas and Clemson

3

Faith

I think the development of faith is a continuing process. You continue to nurture your faith every day through your reverence and quiet time with Him. Once you accept God's grace, you never feel that you've arrived to meet His expectations. You never feel worthy of what Christ has done for you. To me, the greatest thing someone could ever do is lay down his life for others. So I will always feel unworthy of God's gifts.

Without faith, I wouldn't be anything. Faith is what gives me hope every day, knowing we have a promise for eternal salvation after this life ends. I know I don't merit that incredible promise, and I know I fall short on certain days. But I live each day conscious of that commitment I have to God.

My grandmother and Sunday school teachers had a great impact on that. I've been privileged to listen to some great ministers. I've also been blessed to see some great friends in their Christian walk and the continuing development of their faith.

A lot of the men I've been privileged to be with in Bible study have had a lot to do with the development of my faith. It's important to continue to learn and grow as a Christian. One of the best ways to do that is to be in an active study or fellowship.

I feel as a Christian that it's my responsibility to "go ye into all world and preach the gospel." I don't think that necessarily means we have to leave our immediate environment because there are lots of opportunities to spread the word in your community and the areas around it. That being said, I have so much respect for missionaries who go out in the field. However, we also have mission fields right where we live. And we spread the word daily by how we live and conduct ourselves. Depending on how we go about it, we have wonderful opportunities to greatly impact the lives of those around us.

You don't have to beat your chest and proclaim "I'm a Christian" to everyone you meet. But you have to walk the walk, not just talk the talk. Being a Christian has everything to do with how you approach life and the way you treat people.

Your Christianity isn't just about what you say, it is shown by the consistency of how you live your life. I appreciate that in Christians. I feel that when I'm called on to speak to groups that it is God saying, "Here is an opportunity to spread the word." To that end, I believe a lot of our opportunities are Spirit led.

Christian faith is more important than ever. It is the moral fiber of our society, and today, our society is more fragile than ever. If people lived more to Christian ethics and doctrine and had been brought up the way I was privileged to be brought up, I don't think that moral fiber would have become so weakened.

Even in college I had chapel twice a week, in addition to previously having chapel in elementary school and high school. Those were important times. Each chapel started with something spiritually inspirational, and to this day I still remember a lot of it.

There's just so much that can take kids away from the church. I'm so glad I had the opportunity to stay constantly involved. That came from the way I was raised and the faith that was instilled and constantly developed, in me.

I'm not saying I was always the perfect kid in church. I'd crawl under the pews and tickle people's feet. When that happened, grandmother would take me outside and wear me out a little bit and then bring me back in. She was teaching me right from wrong and it made an impression.

Today, many young people in our society are growing up without the necessary values.

How can that happen?

Church has been taken out of school by interpreting laws and "civil rights." What about the rights of those who are victims of violence, racism and other forms of hate born out of a lack of Christian principles.

You look at the massacre at Columbine High School and can see it first hand. As soon as the tragedy was over, the first thing we were encouraged to do was pray. The news showed prayer, the Christian groups at and around the school were welcomed in to help the healing. Yet, if we had prayer in our schools, a lot of situations—perhaps even Columbine—might have been precluded. These are lessons kids need to hear.

I am encouraged today that Young Life, the Fellowship of Christian Athletes and other religious organizations are getting some room on campus. This moral training has been lacking for far too long. This kind of fellowship can and will prevent incidents like Columbine.

That's why I endorse Christian-based organizations. For me, it's been a connecting point to my friends, athletes and coaches. It's also given athletes a tremendous platform to demonstrate, share and spread their faith, especially to those who need it, in particular the kids who are on the edge.

Our society has gotten so permissive. We've even tolerated and been permissive in our judgment of things that would not have been accepted years ago, things that I think have had a way of chipping away at the morals of society, wearing away the crux of Christianity and moral principles.

You can see this permissiveness anywhere. The media is a collection of permissiveness. You can hear words and see acts on television of nudity, violence and bad language. You can't turn on a TV or go to a movie without seeing someone jump in bed with someone else. No, you don't always see the act itself in most cases, but you can figure out what's going on. That's why I encourage the groups I address to turn the TV off because a lot of that is stuff we shouldn't be teaching our kids today.

Don't get me wrong: I'm not against television. There is some very positive stuff on TV, especially on public television and some of the learning-based channels. I watch maybe two hours of TV a week. We know from research that some kids are watching five to six hours of TV a day. The TV has become a babysitter, and often, parents don't know what their kids are watching. A lot of what the kids are watching isn't conducive to becoming strong, responsible young people with a good sense of accountability. Instead, they watch stuff that creates a sense of inquisitiveness in their minds. To me, that is the work of the devil. Certainly, we didn't get to this point overnight, and it doesn't make a lot of sense to me why society continues down this path.

"Wedding day"

As I recall, the day Fisher was to give away his beautiful daughter, Michelle, to be married in Colorado Springs, some of the assistant coaches at the Air Force Academy were making wagers on whether Fisher would make it on time.

Well, I performed the ceremony, so I can say that he did make it on time, though his shirt might have been untucked in the back and his cufflinks were no where to be found.

During the ceremony, I asked, "Who presents this woman to be married to this man?"

The father usually responds, "I do," and maybe mentions the bride's mother as well.

Not Fisher. He went on and on, listing relatives and maybe even some friends. He had his alliterations going and everything—the whole list.

I put my hands in the form of the letter "T."

"Time out, Coach," I said. Everybody laughed, but that's who Fisher is. He wanted everyone who was part of it to get credit.

Fisher is a very unusual person in that what you see is who he is. There is no scam. He is as authentic with a CEO or Air Force general as he is with those who briefly touch his life in everyday tasks. He understands people only as Gifts from God. He knows all people have been created in God's image, so he treats them with respect. His commitment to God and his commitment to Christ are extremely authentic.

Every single morning, Fisher sets aside time for devotion, reading Scripture and prayer. He's very disciplined and methodical about that. His entire life is based on devotion.

That I might have touched a person like Fisher means a lot—for him to say that means something because he does not "blow smoke." I thank God that in some small way, I was able to do that because he impacts so many people. There's a connection among an entire community. The one ripple goes out a long way. I'm not talking only of the thousands of players he has coached. It extends to wherever he goes to speak. With his magnanimous personality, he tells communities what is real to him and what gives his life meaning. What gives his life meaning is the Lord and the people whom God has put in his life.

Ed Beck, minister

4

What about the Children?

You often hear people talking about how kids today "have it so tough" and how it is now "a tougher time than ever to be a kid."

Well, I remember having to work at a young age. I remember never having any "down time" to play video games, worry about dying my hair and getting body piercings or watching television for hours and hours a day—heck, we didn't even have a television until I was a junior in high school.

The only reason it's tougher to be a kid nowadays is because parents have made it easier to shirk responsibility and, more importantly, accountability. Kids don't do chores. They get a car when they turn 16. If you are forking over $20 bills to your child today, they're going to be expecting $20 more next week and $50 next year. We're not making the kids work for it. That leaves the child with no sense of account-ability and no appreciation for what money truly represents— hard work through which money is earned.

There was talk about eliminating the system of giving grades in school recently. What would that accomplish? Take away a child's incentive to achieve, and we will be left with kids who are not only unwilling to achieve, but kids who are unable to achieve because we have not provided the means through which this process takes place. Granted, too much competition and too much focus on winning and losing can ruin any endeavor, making it not just unpleasant, but downright destructive. Kids have to be willing to compete, at least with themselves to improve, and they do need to see where their peers are, if for nothing else but a social measuring stick. Since the real measure of winning or losing isn't by grades, we need to realize that winning and achieving are relative to our children's effort and the input we give them. If your child gets a C in school one semester and a B the next semester, that is improvement—that is winning, even though it's not an A.

Some kids get A's with little effort; some who apply themselves do not. That's just how it works and it's not fair—but neither is life, if you recall. Children will have their "day of A's" when they find their niche or interest, so eliminating a way to measure their success and progress also eliminates a way to gauge aptitude.

If you feed these kids cake for three meals a day, they miss out on the meat-and-potatoes down the road—and I'm talking about work ethic, respect and senses of both responsibility and accountability.

The love and commitment from my mother and grandparents showed me what it means to be a parent.

Of course, I don't know that I realized even half of that when I was growing up back then. However, in hindsight, especially, I see the incredible work they did to raise me under trying circumstances. The most amazing part is that I didn't know the circumstances were that trying. I had all the love I needed. Someone was always there to hug me when I needed it, or to listen when I had a question. They always wanted to hear about my day, what I was learning and what my peers were going through. In that small house, in that small town, I learned an awful lot about life and love.

My grandparents and mother taught me that you must be willing to do whatever you have to for your children.

I pray every day that I will be the proper role model to my children. Having children changes you in a lot of ways. You find a compassion and nurturing kind of love that you never knew existed. An area of your heart is opened up and God allows you to care for these little bodies more than you ever thought possible. You always hear from others when you are getting ready to have kids that "it's 10 times more work than you can even imagine." It's also a million times more rewarding and meaningful than anyone could ever describe in words.

You make decisions about your life—about who you really are and who you should be—when you have children. You are just so humbled that such a miracle could occur. It shows you that only an awesome God could make something like this happen.

I was not the most ideal young person ever raised. I went through difficult times just like anybody. I did a lot of things I'm not proud of, but things happen for a reason. When I was in the Army, I was celebrating with a friend who was in the Navy who had played hockey and football at Harvard.

When he separated from the Navy, we had a party at his house. We had a few drinks early in the afternoon to celebrate his military departure and for me being done with the exams I had taken at the University of Pittsburgh. The social gathering lasted well into the night. I was taking my date home at three in the morning—I should have taken her home sooner.

I was 23 years old and driving a new Chevrolet Super Sport. After I dropped her off, I was driving home on the interstate and fell asleep at the wheel. I came to the place where I was supposed to get off and didn't react fast enough. Instead of doing the smart thing and staying on the interstate, I tried to make the exit anyway. But I hit a cement-based sign and totaled my car. I was lucky I wasn't killed. I was beat up and cut in several places. Fortunately, God spared my life.

That's something I can share with young people—alcohol had a contributing factor to that. There were other factors certainly: The car was hot, it was very late at night and I was going on very few hours of sleep. However, the bottom line was, alcohol was at least a contributing factor. That really opened my eyes, and I've never forgotten that night. I also learned from it. When I got the money from the insurance settlement, I felt like I had to do something good with the money. I didn't deserve a new car, not after what I'd done. So I bought my mother a fur coat. She always had taken so much pride in how she dressed and never had any expensive clothes. After my mother died, the coat has since been passed on to Lu Ann. She doesn't wear it much, what with all the protests over fur and such, but the coat has a special meaning to us.

I didn't drink much after the accident. When Lu Ann and I were married, I had the occasional beer. I'd come in after cutting the grass on Saturday and enjoy a cold beer. When our daughter was born though, it made me think: Is this the kind of influence I want to have on her? Is this the image I want to portray to our children? If I used alcohol in front of my kids, how could I ever correct them if they one day came home under the influence? They would have seen their dad do it, so they'd think it was all right.

There comes a time in every man's life when he has to make decisions. Not drinking has never interfered with a social opportunity, so I don't subscribe to that "social drinking" theory. We have never tolerated alcohol in our home since.

I know I haven't always been the perfect role model for my kids—we all fall short no matter how hard we try—but by the grace of God, I always had the attitude that I would try to be the best role model at every turn. I was always aware of that responsibility. I take that same feeling and determination to be a good role model to every young person who is sent to us at the Air Force Academy by his or her parents. That trust means the world to me. To trust me with their most prized possession is the highest compliment I can be paid. And I value it as I did for our own children at home.

Of course, Lu Ann had a lot more to do with the upbringing of our children than I did. When we were married and she first became pregnant, we made a commitment that as long as I could put some bread on the table and keep milk in the refrigerator, Lu Ann would leave teaching and raise our children.

A mother has the most important job in the world.

If you want to give your children two things—and think of it as being able to give your children ONLY two things—give them these: LOVE and TIME.

In my mind, there are three very important—and often very unmet—needs and wants for young people today.

As I recruit the entire United States I sense this. The number one need is for positive role models. In athletics today, we don't think it's as important as it really is. That's why I support the Fellowship of Christian Athletes and other Christian sports organizations.

Athletes are looked up to and held in reverence. If you're leading in the right way, you can use your role as an athlete to share your faith and to conduct yourself so others can look up to you. Young people today, more than ever before, need positive role models. Statistics show us that since their birth in1987, an overwhelming number of children are lacking a positive role model in their lives. These kids are 13 years old in 2000, so these are very formative years.

I really believe that if you don't give kids positive activities and organizations, they'll find the negative things and get that association and indulge in that. Kids' most basic needs are to be accepted, wanted and loved by a group—to identify. When kids are left out, they get lonesome, so they will look for something for acceptance. That's where kids end up with negative reinforcement groups because the gangs will embrace them and make them a part of their "family." That leads the kids off the right track. They are taught that stealing is okay because it's part of the family. They're taught that hurting other gangs is okay because it helps their gang.

So we have to give them something positive to belong to and that starts with family. If the kids don't find it there, they will find it other places. That had something to do with Columbine. The killers were two young men who were different, who weren't accepted socially. So they found a negative way to combat their lack of love and acceptance: to dress a little differently, to build bombs, and to kill."

These two kids were under the influence of stories told by a young man by the name of Brian Warner.

Let me tell you what I've learned from the Internet about Brian Warner.

Brian Warner grew up and was part of a church and in a youth group. He was a little different and not part of the group. The church group went on an excursion. The youth minister asked the group to pair up and no one paired up with Brian. So, Brian felt rejected and left out. Brian came back for a few months to the youth group meetings but eventually lost interest and disappeared. Not many heard from him. The man who was the youth minister for that group years later became a leader in the church as moral director. One of the kids from the group became a youth minister. One day the church leader was talking to the youth minister, who had been among the kids in that group with Brian Warner.

"Do you know what happened to Brian Warner?" the church leader asked. "You remember him, right?"

"Yes, I do," the youth minister said. "He's changed his name. He's now Marilyn Manson."

Had Brian been accepted by his peers and had positive influences in his life, he might be leading thousands and thousands of young people to Christ. Now, he's leading thousands to hell with what he's teaching kids and how they are absorbing it.

I'm not absolving the kids or their families for this, but at the same time, this horrible influence is out there, and kids are looking to Marilyn Manson and preaching and practicing his teachings. I understand the students who did the shooting at Columbine High School were heavily under the influence of Marilyn Manson's music.

That's a classic example of why kids need to be accepted for who they are. They also have to make an effort.

There's no stronger pressure than that coming from peers. It is the single-greatest force on our young people. Kids are really under unbelievable pressure today. They need more help and more guidance. They're so fragile in this day and age. Yet they are more talented and have access to more learning devices through technological advances.

They still need the basic foundations and values in life that my generation grew up needing. That's why I am grateful to my family and the leaders in my church who influenced me growing up. They were there for us.

A lot of times I felt more comfortable talking to my youth group leaders than my mother or grandparents about certain things. They gave of themselves to us and our church.

That's where athletics can come in. I grew up in a segregated community with rich and poor kids, white kids and black kids. But we were all on the same team. On any real team, you care about your teammates like you would your brother. They all have to be on our team in life.

Young people have to have something to belong to because there are negative forces who prey on the insecure and vulnerable.

The second factor kids crave is family stability. Young people want that in their lives. Unfortunately, today 60 percent of our marriages end in divorce. One out of every four young people in this country lives in a single-parent household! Some 87 percent of these kids live with their mothers. Where have the dads gone?

That's why today the role of coach and teacher—and the team—is more important than ever before. Because the coach or teacher becomes a father figure, sadly perhaps the only one a kid will have in his or her life. Even when there are two parents, the kids can be without a positive role model. Sometimes the only family identification for the young person is belonging to a team.

So much of success is tied to money in our society. People base success on the size of their house and the kind of cars they drive. Therefore, we don't see as much role modeling from the parents as we saw in the past. Kids are dropped off at daycare as babies at seven in the morning and not picked up until six at night. That's a lot of time away from the parents. Who is shaping those kids during that time? That's not to say that there aren't some great daycare providers out there. And it is important for kids to learn socialization among their peers. But for more than 40 hours a week, every week? At what cost to the children and family? How can we equate a dollar value or income to the upbringing of our children?

The third thing that kids need and want is discipline. We think that if we give them the material things, then they will love us more. We think they'll be better if they get what they want. That's not how it is. There's very little depth or substance to that way of thinking. Kids want to know what is right, and they want to do the right thing. That's why I've dedicated 38 years of my life to coaching and teaching because there is such a need. Athletics, in a lot of ways and in a lot of cases, is the last stronghold of discipline we have in this country.

I'm talking always to my daughter about getting my seven-year-old grandson to join the Cub Scouts and then the Boy Scouts. I belonged to the Boy Scouts, though I didn't follow it all the way through. I wish I would have.

These kinds of organizations are important, more now than ever. Young people today need to find an accountability partner. They need an accountability partner more than they need someone who consumes alcohol, does drugs, raises cane or mayhem, or pleases them sexually. Because if you have to face your accountability partner each day or week, it makes you want to tow the line a bit firmer. This is why I endorse the Fellowship of Christian Athletes (FCA) One Way 2-Play program.

It all comes back to parenting. I think it's so important today for the parents to be involved in what the kids are doing. It seems like both parents are working these days, and I suppose that might be necessary, but it can be done without sacrificing the raising of children—otherwise don't bring them into this world. If you have no plans to raise your kids and you and your spouse are going to work 60 hours each a week, you aren't anywhere near the commitment level needed to raise kids. I still think it's best to have one parent stay at home. But I also believe it's more important to simply have a strong commitment to your children.

Sure you take your kids to practice and buy them all the

things they need, but it's also important to be committed to helping them grow and find direction. Praise your kids for what they do well, but show them where they fall short. Just be there for them.

Be there for their school plays and those kinds of things. When my kids were growing up, my wife and I made a commitment to "date night"—not just with each other (which is also important) but to do it with the kids. That gives the kids your full attention and time. Sometimes that meant dinner and a movie or a game. On other occasions it meant staying at home and doing something together there. As the kids grew and we felt each needed more one-on-one attention from each of us, we switched the format. On date night, I'd take our daughter one week and my wife would take our son. We'd switch the next week. We took all of our vacations together, too. We just never felt anything should override the value of family time. Here's something that I think illustrates those thoughts. It's a story a friend e-mailed to me:

One day an expert on time management was speaking to a group of business students. To drive home a point, he used an illustration those students will never forget.

As he stood in front of the high-powered overachievers, he said, "Okay, time for a quiz." He then pulled out a one gallon, wide-mouthed Mason jar and put it on the table in front of him. He then produced almost a dozen fist-sized rocks and carefully placed them, one at a time, into the jar. When the jar was filled to the top and no more rocks would fit inside, he asked, "Is the jar full?"

Everyone in the class answered, "Yes."

Then he asked, "Really?"

He reached under the table and pulled out a bucket of gravel. He dumped some gravel in and shook the jar, causing the pieces of gravel to work themselves down into the space between the big rocks. Then he asked the group once more, "Is the jar full?"

By this time, the class was on to him. "Probably not," one of the students answered.

"Good!" he replied excitedly. He reached under the table and brought out a bucket of sand. He started dumping the sand in the jar. As he poured it in, the sand went into all the spaces between the rocks and the gravel. Once more he asked the question, "Is the jar full?"

"No!" The class shouted in unison.

Once again, he said, "Good!" Then he grabbed a pitcher of water and began to pour it in until the jar was filled to the very brim. Then he looked at the class and asked, "What's the point of this illustration?"

One eager student raised his hand and said, "The point is, no matter how full your schedule is, if you try really hard you can always fit some more things in!"

"No, that's not the point," the speaker replied. "The truth this illustration teaches us is that if you don't put the big rocks in first, you'll never get them in at all. What are the 'Big Rocks in your life? Your loved ones. Your faith. Your education. Your dreams. A worthy cause. Teaching or mentoring others. Doing things that you love. Time for yourself. Your health. Other significant people in your life. Remember to put these big rocks in first, or you'll never get them in at all. If you sweat the little stuff—the gravel and the sand—you'll fill up your life with little things to worry about that don't really matter. You'll never have the real quality time you need to spend on the important stuff—the big rocks. So tonight, or in the morning, when you are reflecting on this short story, ask yourself, 'What are the big rocks in my life?' When you figure that out, put those big rocks in your jar first."

That's a good example.

I'm so proud that both of our children—now very much adults—have based their lives on the teaching of Jesus Christ and God's love. That's the most satisfaction I see when I look at our kids.

My family always supported what I've done. Of course, Lu Ann has been amazing. Joe went with me on a lot of recruiting trips—anywhere there was a McDonald's or Hardees, he was ready to go. That allowed us a lot of time together. Michelle enjoyed football as well. We also spent a lot of time doing the horse thing—she loved to compete in barrel racing. I've tried to be there for them, but there's no doubt that they've made a lot of sacrifices for my career.

Coaching is toughest on the spouses. Lu Ann and I spent a lot of time apart because of my work. We've always done what we can to get the quality family time, so on a lot of occasions that meant them coming along on "work" things.

You never truly accomplish anything by yourself.

The best moment for me as a parent was when both kids told me they had accepted Christ at an FCA camp. Our son, Joe, has been a "huddle" group leader for the Fellowship of Christian Athletes (FCA). At Air Academy High School, Joe started a Fellowship of Christian Athletes group. He went to a teacher, Glen Hoyt, and asked him if he could meet in a Bible study with the group Joe had formed. In 1986, we hosted it at our home. The kids would come over each week at six a.m. Lu Ann would put out juice, fruit, donuts or muffins for the kids. Joe told us that the Bible study really impacted his social life and how he handled himself on the weekends when he was out with his friends.

When Joe went off to college at Clemson, Cal McCombs—who was on our staff and whose son Will took over the Bible study when Joe graduated—hosted the kids at his house. It's gone now from Coach McComb's house to

Coach Miller's house, who also has a child involved. It's just incredible to see how that's perpetuated itself in the past 14 years on our campus.

Joe had an outstanding high school career and had the option of playing college football or baseball. Joe was very active in Athletes in Action in college and then was instrumental in starting baseball chapels for the teams he was on after he turned professional in baseball. I was disappointed for Joe that he didn't make it to the major leagues. He had the foundation to make it. There were so many times that Joe was on the verge of making it to the major leagues. Each time, a trade happened or something else that left him as the odd man out. But God apparently had other plans for Joe's life because Joe missed almost two consecutive seasons with injuries and this threw him off schedule.

However, Joe had the capabilities to deal with it very well. Besides, as Lu Ann said, "That was God's plan for Joe. Who knows? If he would have made the major leagues, maybe he would not become the person he is." That Lu Ann, she's got it all figured out! However, her point is sound: Joe didn't have to make it to the major leagues to complete himself as a person. He has everything he needs in his faith and family. I know that he would have done a fine job as a good role model and a witness for God had he made it to the highest level. However, not making the majors didn't diminish his effort or ever affect his faith. He has his own business now which is founded on Christian principles.

Our daughter, Michelle, is just an amazing person. I'm so proud of her. She gave up her teaching career to devote her life to raising her four children. That comes from the unconditional love she received from her mother. Seeing the kind of mother Michelle has become to her children is such an inspiration to me.

Research tells us that families who go to church together have fewer problems. Communities that have strong churches and youth groups have happier, better functioning families, and then that extends into the community.

That's what's wrong with the nation today; We've lost the importance of family and lost the importance of the family concept. That's morally weakened our country.

5

Sports and Life

Sports were always a big part of my upbringing—though my mother and my grandparents, whom I lived with, didn't know much about sports or have much interest in that direction.

We didn't have a television until I was in high school. I didn't read the paper much, but I listened to a lot of baseball and football games on the radio. When Cheraw's own Tom Brewer played for the Boston Red Sox, I'd rush into our house before the game started and turn on that radio. I really enjoyed the radio as a medium. It left a little to the imagination and that made you think. I could smell the hot dogs and feel the stickiness of the seat from the soda that had spilled. I could smell the hide on the baseball. By the sound of the hit, I could tell how hard the ball was hit, if it was going a long way or if the pitcher had jammed the batter inside.

Sports is a great learning device to promote love among all races and nationalities.

The era in which I grew up had some of the most strained race relations of all time. There weren't a lot of minorities in our town when I was growing up, so sports helped me learn to love men of other colors and nationalities.

I had a lot of minority friends. Back then there was segregation, so the black kids would go to other schools. They were my friends, so I'd go watch some of their games. I got to see the ugly face of racism up close several times, and it just sickened me. I never understood the mentality of someone having a different color skin being different or inferior. They loved like us, cared like us and bled like us.

Still, that didn't stop the hate on occasions. I remember one time we were playing a team from a nearby town. On that team was a black kid. That was the first time we had played a team that had a black kid on it. One of our kids followed the black kid to a water fountain and picked a fight with him, bloodying his nose. I really turned on my friend because I knew that was wrong. I knew he picked the fight only because of the kid's race. I stood up to my friend and told him what I thought about what he did.

So I credit sports with helping me learn the evil of racism and the importance of loving all of our brothers, regardless of skin color or ethnic background.

Nothing can teach you more about life than competitive athletics. Life is not all roses all the time. You have your ups and downs. You have to overcome adversity. Every Saturday I talk to my team before we go on the field. "We will have adversity. I wish I could tell you what it is. But how we handle it will tell people a lot about our character."

Sometimes you overcome it; sometimes you don't. The point is you have to overcome adversity in life. I can't think of anything that teaches you more than sports. You learn skills, build yourself physically and mentally, learn how to compete (sportsmanship) and how to get along with people.

I've been blessed in my career to be surrounded by such capable and wonderful people. I've never had a lot of bad attitudes around me. We haven't had a lot of big egos, and we don't tolerate them. I have never worked with anyone I didn't like or didn't respect. I've had some strong personalities, but never anyone I couldn't work with. Athletics brings out the best in people. It teaches you teamwork.

At the entrance to our dressing room, our players see a sign every day that reads, "You make the difference." In forming a team, I impress upon them that there's no "I" in the spelling of the word team. You have to immerse yourself in the team concept. Everyone has a role, from a backup to a trainer to an administrator—the bus driver, the equipment managers. Everyone has a role, and no role is more important than anyone else's role. I honestly know that to be true.

How each person accepts a role—and the pride taken in that role—determines our success.

That's why it's so important for me to let everybody know how much I value their roles and their input, and how much I appreciate them. The attitude they have toward their jobs or roles is going to determine the success of the team. So it's not just the team that wins on Saturday. There are a lot of people off the field who made that happen.

Everyone has a role and a job to do. The pride you take in that job will determine the pride of the organization and the success that comes.

People talk to me and say, "Your team this, your team that." This isn't my team; it's our team. Certainly, I am the head coach and someone has to ultimately make a decision that is hopefully best for the team—and that responsibility is mine. However, our staff knows they have the freedom to recommend and make any suggestions as long as they sincerely believe it's best for the team.

Unfortunately, when the team wins, the head coach gets more credit than he deserves, and when the team loses, the head coach certainly must accept the responsibility for losing. I understand that, and it goes with the territory and the job. But the coaches on the staff here do feel they have a responsibility. Our coaches know that when I give them a responsibility, I'm not going to stand looking over their shoulders telling them what to do or how to it. I hired them because they are good people and good coaches. That's why it's important to surround yourself with good people. Success is determined by having good people. I really think we've been blessed to have not just good coaches in X's and O's, but good family people, who care about their families and the kids they coach.

Our coaches and players like each other and care about each other. That's also something that will not always come naturally or automatically. It's something you have to work at. That's what team chemistry is all about. I'm a real big believer in chemistry among team members and the coaching staff. That's why I believe you can take talent that might be deemed a bit inferior and whip a team with a couple of dozen Parade All-Americans—if you have the chemistry and you are good in the intangibles. When players are playing for the guy next to them and everyone is pulling on the same end of the rope and not trying to draw attention to himself, there is a much better working environment. That all comes out on the field, sooner or later.

"Hanging our hopes on a Fish"

When head football coach Ken Hatfield needed to turn around the Air Force football program, he decided to put in the Wishbone and have Fisher DeBerry join the staff. Hatfield went in and saw then Athletic Director Colonel John Clune in Clune's office.

"John, I've made some decisions about the program." Hatfield said.

"I'm all ears," Clune replied.

"Well, we're going to go to the Wishbone on offense," Hatfield said, "and I'm going to hire this guy from Appalachian State, Fisher DeBerry, to install it. He's a real expert."

"Okay, Kenny, let me get this straight," Clune says. "We're going to run the Wishbone and hire Fisher ... someone from Appalachian State to install it?"

"Yep," Hatfield answers.

"We're going to have to talk about this later," Clune says, "because I have to get a drink."

Obviously, it worked out more than all right.

One of the things Fisher said one time really stuck with me. In 1992, Air Force was 7-4 heading into the Liberty Bowl against Mississippi. Air Force lost, 13-0.

After bowl games, everyone mills around the field because of the presentation of trophies and MVP awards. Fisher saw me and by that point, I had been on the beat since 1985, so he knew me well. He came up to me on the field and pointed at the scoreboard.

"Look at that scoreboard," he said.

"Yes?" I said. "What about it."

"See that zero under 'Air Force'?" Fisher asked.

"Yeah," I answered.

"I guarantee you that you won't see that again as long as I'm the head coach at Air Force," Fisher said.

You look back through the records since then and Fisher was right. That really shows his competitive side. Plus, he was able to back it up.

I think what DeBerry's done at the Air Force Academy is one of the most amazing things in sports, especially in college athletics.

I covered him for 14 full seasons, through 1998, covering almost every game. I've been in this business 25 years now, and I've never had so much difficulty trying to maintain my objectivity. Fisher is such a wonderful, good-hearted person that you find yourself rooting for him, even though you aren't supposed to. There were things I actually had to do to guard against being such a "homer."

Randy Holtz, sportswriter, the Rocky Mountain News

"Did you hear the one about..."

The thing that I think most about when I think of Fisher

is the guy who hired Coach DeBerry and me—the late Colonel John Clune, who was the athletic director at the Air Force Academy.

Since I've been the baseball coach at Notre Dame, I've had a picture of Fisher and Colonel Clune on the wall of my office. Colonel Clune hired me at the Academy in 1988.

When I first got to the Academy, I was just in awe of it—the whole place is such a neat environment.

I thought the world of John Clune—not just because he hired me, but because of who he was. Shortly after I arrived at the Academy, Fisher taught me how the Academy worked. Here was this established football coach taking all his time and energy to show this young, new baseball coach the ropes, what we needed to know as coaches at a military academy, and so on—it was a gesture I've never forgotten. I just couldn't believe the interest and excitement Fisher showed in me and the baseball program.

I have admired Fisher for so many reasons. You hear the story about how Fisher got his first head coaching job at Air Force, and you are really impressed by how he was so prepared for it and knew so much on both sides of the ball. I used to watch his practices and just marveled at how organized they were and how meticulous the planning was. Those coaches know the cadets don't have a lot of time to waste, and they make the most of every minute, which I think the players also greatly appreciate.

I admired the balance among his faith, family and his profession. Everyday I went to work, I felt like I was going to school because I could learn by watching a guy like Fisher DeBerry do his job. I really looked at him as a mentor. To this day, when I get mail—and I get a huge stack of it every day as the coach at Notre Dame—the moment I see that "Air Force Football" logo, I rush to it and tear it open. Fisher's kind words always pick me up. To me, Fisher represents all that is good about college sports.

Our friendship has grown to the point where I consider Fisher one of my best friends and always will.

It's funny because college football coaches across the country have so much respect for him. The football coaches here at Notre Dame just marvel at Fisher. He has a reputation of being THE coach who gets more out of the talent he has than anybody else in the country. How many of Fisher's kids are recruited nationally? Yet he gets these kids, and they can beat anyone. What he's done at the Academy is an amazing thing.

There was a period of something like six years where there wasn't a single change on Fisher's staff. I was amazed that he could harbor such loyalty among his staff.

On Wednesdays, Fisher would speak at the Quarterback Club luncheon after being introduced by Colonel Clune. I attended every single one of those things. I just enjoyed listening to Fisher, and I learned from his public speaking. Plus, Colonel Clune and Fisher had this awesome back-and-forth humor kind of thing. When Colonel Clune would introduce Fisher, he'd always have some funny barb, like something about Fisher being from a small town in the South or something about Fisher's accent. Well, Fisher would get up there and zing Colonel Clune about being from the Northeast or something else humorous. It was almost like a vaudeville act, and the audience just loved it. Colonel Clune would occasionally come by my office in the morning before the Quarterback Club luncheons, asking if I "had a good one" to get Fisher with because Fisher had really zinged him the week before. That was his and Fisher's way of showing affection for each other. They were very, very close.

What a great, fun place that was to work, with positive people who deeply cared for each other, just like a family.

Paul Mainieri, head baseball coach, Notre Dame

6

Coaching is Teaching

Coaching is no Utopia. We have some things better here than other programs, but we're not perfect. However, you don't focus on the negative things. You focus on the positives and what you do have. We have quality people and good coaches. We have the military training for our players. A lot of people could view that as a negative. We treat it as something completely positive.

The people I have a great admiration for are the ones who I see have the greatest obligations. I tell our assistant coaches that I hope they feel they have the best assistant coaching job in America. I hope you are excited about coming to work each day to serve these fine young people here and being associated with the coaching brothers we have on this staff. If you're not and you don't feel like this is the best job, I will help you find the right job for you. There is no "perfect" coaching job in the world or in life. But wherever I am, I will believe I have the best job in America.

I do think the Air Force Academy is the best coaching job in America. I think the Academy offers the best education in America. I believe Colorado is the best place in the world to live, and I'll go to my grave saying that and believing that. If I ever don't feel that I can say that, then it's time to move on somewhere else.

You can't expect people to believe in and support your program if you don't completely believe in it. You can't expect them to work hard and be positive if you aren't.

You can go to any college in the nation and hear assistant coaches finding all kinds of fault with their program or college. A lot of coaches believe Florida State, Notre Dame, Penn State and Nebraska are the best places to coach—that everything is perfect. However, I've talked to coaches from those schools, and they all have challenges to overcome and adversity to meet. There just isn't any Utopias.

On our staff, we simply won't tolerate a negative attitude.

I've talked about character, and that's one of the most important things we look for when we're bringing another coach on board. It's important to surround yourself with people of great character.

You'll find that people with great character are unfailingly positive and loyal as well. That's important. In my mind, the greatest sin is a person who has lost enthusiasm for what he or she is doing, yet still goes through the motions and does it. Sometimes you have to have the courage to move on and find something else better for you.

You are going to be able to breed character only if you have character. That is, winning is important, but taking shortcuts to win is not what the essence of coaching is all about. You are trying to teach people through athletics, the right way to live. That's why wins and losses aren't the overriding factor. I know men of overwhelming character who lost their jobs because they weren't willing to compromise their character and sell out their ideals and values at all costs. They lost games or seasons because they would not take shortcuts. That hardly makes them losers in my book—it makes them winners.

Don't get me wrong, you have to win a certain number of

games to keep your job. However, if you have everything else in place that matters—character, good people, a system that you believe in and continually build on—you should win far more games than you lose.

Character has to be the rock solid foundation of any organization. You have to have a philosophy and foundation of high character to build on. If you don't have that, the foundation is going to be shaky. You have to base your foundation on doing what's right. We have only one rule in our program: "Do what's right." Our players are mature enough to know what's right.

As the head coach, you must show good character and that has to do with being concerned not only with your assistants' jobs on the field, but their lives off the field. You have to see that professional success goes with personal success. The happiness and enthusiasm from their home lives translates on the field, as does discontentment and unhappiness.

So, I realize I need to keep the personal and professional needs my coaches have in mind.

I did miss some of my children's upbringing because of the long hours I put in at the office. I learned from that, and I am not about to let that happen to my staff. So I insist in the afternoon after practice that our coaches go home. I don't want them staying at the office and then going home to see that their kids are already in bed. I wasn't at home as much as I should have been, so I don't let them stay at work all night. It's important for them to be home in the evening and have a meal with their wives and children. They need to be active in the raising of their kids and building and nurturing their relationship with their wives. I wasn't smart enough as a young assistant coach to realize that, so I'd be at the office from six in the morning until midnight.

That's not going to happen with my staff. You work that

many hours and you're not that effective, simply from becoming tired and burned out or the emotional loss you feel from missing out on what your family is doing without you there. No job is worth sacrificing the heart of your family over.

I've always had an interest and appreciation for the medical field, especially doctors and nurses. Doctors give so much of themselves to their practice. I have a lot of respect for them, but they tend to ruin their own health to help others. We take doctors and policemen for granted, yet they are there all the time for us. We have to respect these people and realize the sacrifice they make for us. We take them for granted and then when something goes wrong, we're on the phone calling them to help us out. When they make one error, we're all over them, yet the rest of us can get away with making a mistake every day. Our sense of accountability and responsibility has become very misguided through the years.

Here's a poem given to me by a coaching friend early in my career. It speaks about the influence we have:

To Any Athlete

There are little eyes upon you and they're watching night and day
and there are little ears that quickly take in every word you say.
There are little hands all eager to do anything you do,
and a little boy who's dreaming of the day he'll be like you.
You're the little fellow's idol, you're the wisest of the wise;
In his little mind about you, no suspicions ever arise.
He believes in you devoutly, holds all that you say and do;
he will say and do in your own way when he's a grown-up like you.
There's a wide-eye little fellow who believes you're always right,
and his ears are always open, and he watches day and night.
You are setting an example every day in all you do,
for the little boy who's waiting to grow up to be just like you.

That poem shows that we have an impact on people—negative or positive in whatever we do. We have to make sure it is positive—that's part of the responsibility. Some little boy wants to be like me and that can be scary. I know I grew up to be like my high school coaches. Honestly, I can see so much of them in me. Did they know the affect they were having? Probably not, but a lot of people at any level are in coaching because of the impact their coaches had on them. Never underestimate or fail to be aware of the influence you are having with your every action and word.

Coaching is a privilege, but with this privilege comes a great responsibility for this role model we present.

When you coach, you have to be yourself. Young coaches will say, "I'm going to be like Joe Paterno, Tom Osborne or Bobby Bowden." There's only one Joe Paterno and only one Tom Osborne and only one Bobby Bowden. They are great coaches and more importantly, great people. Players wanted to play for them because they knew Joe, Tom and Bobby cared about them. Still, anyone getting into coaching has to be himself or herself and carve a personal path—and, hey, that's great.

To be a good coach you have to be an excellent teacher because being a coach means being able to teach the players to perform different things.

Coaching is a calling. It's something that comes from deep within. You can't do it for ego or money, or clout, or social approval. The first thing, you have to have is a sincere interest in young people and the desire to help them succeed and grow. You have to be patient. You have to care about them—that's the foundation of why you coach. It's all about teaching.

Coaching isn't for everyone. In coaching, especially the past decade or so, the expectations of the fans and boosters are so high. There's something out there that I call "instant-winning syndrome." No one is willing to grow with the program, so a lot of good coaches are lost—potentially outstanding coaches—because of the quick-fix attitude.

At the high school level, parents lose patience. At the college level, fans and boosters lose their understanding of the process, and the coach also gets frustrated. Building a good program is a lot like life: It is a journey, and you have to be in it for the long haul. It's not going to happen overnight.

Occasionally, you'll see someone step in and take over a 3-7 team and go 7-3 in his first season. More often than not, his second year is back around .500 or even 3-7 again. So maybe the coach who was pushed out had left the program in better shape than anyone thought. Perhaps the new guy isn't the genius everyone thought he was the first year. That's not fair to either coach—the new one or the one who is gone.

One of the faults in young coaches is that they see coaches doing something, or they see something a coach had success with against them—and then they change their system. Not that we don't steal ideas because very little is original at this point—and they copy it. Sometimes coaches see something on TV in the pros and use it. You have to have a system that you believe in. Of course, you adjust that system and tweak it, but you can't throw out your entire wardrobe just because you get a haircut. As the system needs adapting, you do it, but you don't throw the entire system out because of one game. You try to improve the system, so that whatever stopped you, won't stop you again. You can't change systems every year, but some coaches do. When that happens, they get frustrated. Kids have to work on one system and understand it.

Our players believe so strongly in the option and an outstanding defense and our coaches have done such a good job of selling it to them that it would be out of the realm of consistency to shift systems in mid-flight and expect that same trust to be there.

One of the things you quickly learn as a coach is that you don't want to make the same mistake twice—especially since there is such a fine line between winning and losing. You always seem to remember the games you lost more than the games you won. And that's even truer of coaches who win a lot more than they lose.

We've developed something we call our "football bible," which we use to anticipate situations that are going to occur. It tells us what to do when facing certain situations and schemes.

On Sundays, we watch the film from the previous day's game, and it can be frustrating. We'll see something that went wrong and say, "Look at this—all we had to do was…" But in the heat of battle, you don't always use all the resources you have or think of all the possible scenarios and options. That's why it's a big help to have that "football bible" on my hip throughout the game.

It's ironic but some of our greatest successes have been born out of our toughest moments. When you stub your toe, you want to figure out how to avoid that in the future—you become more determined to come back and not let it happen again. To become a chairman or manager, you have to get up one more time than you are knocked down.

We, as with many staffs, spend a lot of time after the season evaluating every phase of our game, how we can improve it and how we can avoid mistakes from the previous season. Certainly, there are many ways to skin a cat, so you have to be open to change and anything else that will enhance your chances of improving each year.

Coaching is teaching players to do their jobs the right

way. We constantly tell our players, "There's only one way to do it—the right way." So if we don't do it right, we'll do it over and over again.

The foundation of this program is, "Do what's right." Try as hard as we might, certainly we don't do that always. But you always ask yourself: "If I make this decision, will it better our football program?" If the answer is yes, then you do it. If not, you ask someone else or bring it to me. That's just like life, and it's an attitude that I demand be practiced on and off the field.

We believe very strongly in repetition. We believe you never run a play in a game that you haven't run hundreds of times—correctly—in practice.

The best teacher has to be a good example. If you're not enthused as a teacher, you can't expect your players to be enthused about the approach, subject matter or direction. As coaches, we love the challenge of helping young people get from one level to another and do some things they didn't even think they could do, see them overcome mental obstacles.

Looking back, I guess I went into coaching because athletics is the only thing about which I knew anything. I grew up near the baseball and football fields and played every available minute I could. During my most formative years I had role models in my community and in college, and most of them I met through sports.

People have to understand that I was not a great athlete. I made all-state and played in all-star games, and competed in college. But I was not outstanding. What I had was a love for the game, whether it was baseball, basketball, football, track or whatever. Make no mistake, though, I was mediocre. I remember telling someone that I was mediocre and Coach Jim Brakefield overheard me.

"For you to say that you were a mediocre player is an insult to mediocre players everywhere," Brakefield chimed in. "In fact, it's an insult to the word mediocrity."

He said it with a smile, but it painted an accurate picture of my abilities. Still, I always hustled and I always wanted to help the team. If we needed a pitcher, I was the pitcher. I didn't have the best hands or speed in the world, but if the football team needed a receiver, that's what I did, and I could catch the ball a little bit. I didn't throw well enough to be a great quarterback, but when the team needed a quarterback, I played it. Coaches love team-first players.

We have teamwork up and down at the Academy. I tell my players all the time, "Maybe we aren't as strong, quick, talented or fast, and maybe we don't measure up to the powerhouses in a lot of ways. But what we can do is out-hustle our opponent."

The Lord has given us all one thing—the ability to hustle. How much we hustle and how hard we play is going to determine—more than anything else—how successful we're going to be.

We don't believe we're going to lose any games. We might run out of time, but we aren't going to lose. We're going to go in believing we can win every game we play. We're going to be prepared to do that—and that is our job as coaches.

I coach because I want to have an impact on young people's lives. I had a high school player, Larry Nunnery, who is now the CEO of a very successful corporation in Chicago. He was recognized recently by the University of South Carolina as an outstanding alumnus. In the news release, he mentioned the impact that I had on him when he was a high school player and said that he built on some of the foundations I gave him. That means so much.

Even when you have something deemed "successful," I

don't think you ever get completely satisfied. You can't say that one thing determines success. It's the relationships. It's the high moments and the low moments. Sometimes success comes from losing—a setback. You learn a lot about yourself and your relationships after your setbacks, especially the more severe ones.

I don't think success is a quantitative thing. You can't say, "If I work this many hours, I'll have this certain level of success." So many different things determine success. You have to be lucky and the ball has to bounce your way at times—though, if you work hard and do things right, more often than not you'll make your own luck. You have to have great people around you.

If you call our players "overachievers," they are insulted. At the same time, we have to face the reality that a lot of them aren't recruited or contacted by Ohio State, Texas, BYU, Mississippi State, Notre Dame, Virginia Tech—teams that are highly ranked, but also teams that we have beaten.

That's one of the best parts of coaching here—beating those teams. Because you know your athletes weren't as highly regarded as those other schools' recruits coming out of high school. Maybe our kids didn't have the athleticism or skill level to meet the "athletic standards" of the top-ranked schools, but our kids have a lot of pride and want to play and want to prove to people they can play. When you put people like that in that kind of environment, a lot can happen.

You can win a lot of football games with great, impeccable character. That's also what this institution stands for.

Our players live under an honor code. This code of ethics is based on "integrity above all."

One lie leads to another. I've seen it happen time and again. Lying is a shortcut. Nothing good can come from lying. Liars start with one lie, misrepresenting something; then it is justified with another lie. This keeps escalating, and the lies keep mounting.

We had consequences for lying in our home in Cheraw. My mother would wash my mouth out with soap if I lied or used profanity. That was the worst tasting soap you could ever imagine. It got to the point where if I thought of profaning or telling a tale, I'd go dry-mouthed and remember blowing soap bubbles the last time I did it. It all goes back to a simple rule: Do what's right.

That's why I'm so proud to serve at an institution that has such an admirable foundation.

We don't "work" to get players eligible or get any special favors from the professors. These kids don't want or need that because they are here to be challenged, not for a free ride. We don't cheat, and the players can take that honor code experience with them for life. When they look back later in life, that's what they will take great pride in. That's why corporate America pays big, big bucks to hire people who have graduated from the United States Air Force Academy. Of course, it also helps that these are talented people. They learn a lot from their time on active duty and in athletics. They've had tremendous experience, and their people-skills are outstanding. From their time on active duty, they have skills that any corporation is seeking.

However, what separates these young men and women from other people applying at the same job—perhaps who have good credentials—is that our graduates have lived under the honor code. That's an issue of credibility and character.

More than anything else, "Success in coaching is not measured in the number of wins and losses, but the real success is the men who your players become as they move on."

The real success for me is getting letters from kids I coached saying I had a positive impact on their lives. Getting letters and E-mails from former players means so much. Plus, we have a lot of former players come visit and eat at our house or come to our games. I like to see the exciting things they're doing with their lives, especially the ones who are building their own families. I'm proud of the ones in the Air Force and the ones who have moved on to careers in corporate America.

At the Academy, the greatest pride I get is when those guys throw their hats in the air at graduation, not when they cross the goal line on a football field. Don't get me wrong, I'm happy for the players, the assistant coaches and myself when a young man scores a touchdown, but it's about something much bigger.

Another reason I coach is it helps keep me young. I weigh less now than I did when I played in college. I'm not boasting—and Lu Ann might not be feeding me that well (I feel another slap upside the head coming). Coaching has inspired me to stay in shape.

I also coach because I want to give something back for all that was given to me. If it weren't for my coaches, I probably would be back working in a mill. I've seen a lot of kids I grew up with who went the other route, choosing not to learn lessons from their teachers and coaches and never learning what it means to be part of a team.

Coaching also has given me a lot of opportunities to travel and meet people. I guess I'll stay in coaching until the powers that be think I'm too old.

Coaching at the Academy has allowed me to meet several presidents. President Bush always made me feel so good at the White House. What a great man and person he is, in addition to someone who sacrificed a good part of his life for his country.

I was at a meeting for the American Football Coaches

Association a few years back. President Bush was there and he called me over, remembering me from the times we were at the White House to receive the Commander-in-Chief's Trophy.

On President Bush's staff was one of our former players at the Academy, Mike Gould, who will pin on General very soon. President Bush mentioned what a great young man Mike was, and I was as proud as a father. In the summer of 2000, Mike's son came to the Academy and plans to play football for us. That's another honor, Mike knows me and our program and trusts that his son will be fine here as he matures and grows.

President Clinton has been very gracious to us during our trips to the White House. And President Reagan was always very personable. He has such a commanding presence and charisma about him.

We honored Senator Strom Thurmond during our visit to Washington in 2000. We honored him with the White Award for his great career serving this country and his support of the armed forces. The man is 97 years old, and he stood up to receive his award. He recognized the fact that I was from his home state of South Carolina, which made me proud. I'm also proud of what he's done for South Carolina and for the United States. Without his glasses, he stood up there and read his acceptance speech. I thought that was impressive.

"All right guys, break it up"

When Coach DeBerry was thinking about leaving coaching after Coach Jim Brakefield retired at Appalachian State, I went and talked to him. Fisher was getting ready to move his stuff out of the football office. I knew how much he loved coaching and being around young people.

"I just don't think that's the right thing to do," I said.

"I think it might just be the time for me to get out," Fisher said.

Since I felt so close to him, I was concerned. I knew a fair amount about football and coaching from my own experience and that of my father, who was an assistant coach at the Citadel when Bobby Ross was the head coach there. So I kind of knew what Fisher was going through.

A few months later, of course, Fisher was invited to the Air Force Academy—not to interview for a job, but to help them set up the wishbone offense. Not long after he went back to Appalachian, Air Force came calling and offered him a job. I was glad he accepted and the rest is history.

I believe one of the reasons Fisher has been so successful is that he was a defensive assistant and also defensive coordinator before moving to the offense. The teams on which I coached with Fisher were a little ahead of our time in terms of running the triple-option offense. Part of the reason for that was Fisher's defensive experience—he knew the best way to defense it and the best way to attack the defense.

I was also able to play for him at Appalachian State. I learned first-hand how he created a lot of enthusiasm, particularly one day. We were finishing up a scrimmage at spring practice. We were on the one-yard line and wanted to finish with a touchdown on the last play. We broke the huddle. Fisher went to the defense and told the defensive end, "We're going to run the ball right over you. We're going to knock you into the back of the end zone." He said that over and over, just working the player and his defensive teammates into a frenzy. I know that was calculated and Fisher wanted to motivate the player.

Well, we snapped the ball, and every guy on the defense ran to that hole. We were knocked back about three yards. Everyone was so fired up, the whole team, 90 guys, just started going after each other, offense vs. defense. Well, Fisher—a very young assistant coach then—didn't plan on that being the result as he just wanted to motivate someone. He did, but as the players went at it, I could see him just shrinking away in the background. The head coach, Coach Brakefield, came over and made us run 40 laps, thanks to Fisher's enthusiasm!

Not only was I blessed to play with Fisher, I was on his staff at the Air Force Academy before taking the head coaching job at East Tennessee State. My seven years at the Academy with him and the rest of the staff was a very special time in my family's life. He has surrounded himself with so many great people. There's something very special going on out there.

The reason it's worked at the Academy is that Coach DeBerry is such a natural fit for the Academy. He's such a positive individual. He's not someone who dwells on the negatives that some people focus on. You have to deal with some things at the Academy that you just don't have to deal with at "normal" universities. Yet, Fisher is always selling the positives. He truly believes in what the Academy represents and that is displayed so much in his character and the person he is. As a young person who played for him, I was able to see that Coach is such a winner in life itself. What you see is what you get with Coach DeBerry.

It never mattered who we played against or where we were playing because Coach DeBerry had a great way of making our players believe we were supposed to win. That trickled down through the entire coaching staff and the team. That's part of what made it so special. We had great kids to coach out there. It's a very special young person that attends the academy—someone who is a cut above. They had a great influence on my son while we were there.

Coach has really made the Air Force Academy the premier football program among service academies. It wasn't a long time ago that young men coming out of high school who wanted to play college football for a military academy automatically went to West Point or the Naval Academy. That has changed, and it is because of Coach DeBerry. It didn't stop there either: We beat Notre Dame several times. We also beat heavily favored Ohio State.

I really see Coach DeBerry as a very special person in my life. My wife and I and our kids are very close to Coach and his family. I really treasure the times I had with him, especially when we'd be out recruiting in South Carolina and visit his mother or grandmother. His influence on me was profound.

Paul Hamilton, Head Coach, East Tennessee State

"That's Fisher"

There's an old saying, "What you see is what you get."

With Fisher DeBerry, that is the absolute truth. He's no phony. He's the genuine article. I don't think you can find many people like him. Many times when a person reaches the kind of achievement and success that Fisher has, they forget where they've come from, and they take themselves too seriously. One thing about Fisher is that even though he's been the national coach of the year and set the record for winning at the Academy, he hasn't changed at all. Sure he's matured and gotten wiser, but he has that same, solid Christian character that he's always had. He's just one of the great men of faith who has kept his priorities in the right order and because of that, the Lord has honored him.

When I was the head coach at Carson-Newman, Fisher was at Wofford College working with Jim Brakefield as Jim's assistant coach. We went down in the preseason of 1972 to Wofford and worked out. We did some drills and scrimmaged with Wofford for a good while, and we had a great afternoon of two teams getting after each other.

That next year at Carson-Newman, we went on to play for the National Championship. Not long after that Jim and Fisher moved to Appalachian State. They had great success there. I really got to know Fisher through the American Football Coaches Association where we'd get together and talk X's and O's.

We had very similar philosophies on coaching, using wide line splits, moving the ball and how to defense that. We had some fun times.

When Jim decided to retire at Appalachian State, Fisher gave them my name as a possible replacement, and I went to interview. One of my main missions was to visit with Fisher and find out why he wasn't taking the job as head coach. He was very established there as the offensive coordinator, and I thought he'd do a great job as the head coach. Or, if I got the job, I wanted him to be on the staff. However, he told me he was stepping away from football.

"I'm a little disenchanted with coaching, and I probably don't need to be in this profession," he said.

"If you stay here and coach, I'll take this job," I said. "But I don't want to take it if you aren't going to be on the staff."

"No, I'm taking a break," Fisher said. "I'm tired of some parts of the job, so I'm going to step away from coaching a little bit."

On top of that, I couldn't bring in my own staff because there was a freeze on salaries in the state educational system at the time. So I'd have to either take the rest of the staff or wait until they chose to find other jobs. Kenny Rucker was at Appalachian, and I would've been happy to have had him on the staff. But, certainly, I wanted to bring in some of my own assistants. Still, I didn't know if it would be the right place for me, especially since Fisher was going into teaching again full-time and wouldn't be on staff.

I left to go back to Iowa on Wednesday—I was the assistant head coach at Iowa State at that time. I was supposed to let Appalachian State know by Friday if I was going to take the job.

So I flew back to Des Moines, Iowa and drove to Ames, Iowa. I stopped by my office the night I got in and was checking my mail when the phone rang. It was the athletic director at the University of Richmond in Virginia.

"I hear you might be the someone we're looking for," the athletic director said.

I agreed to meet with their president that Friday, so I called Appalachian State to see if I could push their deadline back to Monday. I called Fisher a final time to see if he'd change his mind about coming back to coaching if I took the Appalachian State job.

"I'm going to teach and stay here, but I'm not going to coach," Fisher said. "I have to get out for a while."

I met with the Richmond president at the Des Moines airport and then went to Richmond and accepted the job. Three months later, Ken Hatfield brought Fisher out to the Air Force Academy to show Ken how to install the Wishbone.

It was amazing the way it worked out. I ended up with a job that was perfect for me. And a month after Fisher visited the Academy, Ken Hatfield called to offer him a job because one of his assistants had left unexpectedly. So it worked out well for the both of us. The impression he made on me as to his character, by stepping away from coaching at Appalachian State, is something I will never forget.

Fisher helped Ken put Air Force on the map and then into the national picture, winning bowl games and beating Notre Dame. Fisher took over and has done just an amazing job. What's even more incredible is to see the kind of job offers Fisher has turned down to stay at the Academy. Some of these jobs doubled his Academy salary—one I knew of would have tripled his wages. A lot of coaches break their contracts to leave. You just don't find many guys like Fisher. He just tells the colleges that call him, "Thank you. I'm honored, but I have a commitment to the Air Force Academy."

Fisher is so loyal to the Academy. He sees the class and caliber of the young men who come to school there. He's highly organized, and he takes those young men in as if they were his own kids. He's an outstanding fit for the Air Force Academy.

When Fisher got the job at the Academy, he hired Kenny Rucker, who was on my staff at Richmond. When Richmond realigned and went down to Division I-AA, Fisher called and asked me if I wanted to join his staff and get back to the Division I-A level. I had so much respect for Fisher and the military academies—having been in the Marines myself—that I thought it was a great opportunity. I've always thought greatly of the Air Force Academy. My wife, Barbara, and I went out and visited with Fisher. I had a burning desire to get back to the Division I-A level. But I had a year left on my contract at Richmond. Just like Fisher, I knew I couldn't have any integrity if I broke my contract.

Fisher has had so many great coaches on his staff. The head coaches at Ohio (Jim Grobe), Navy (Charlie Weatherbie), East Tennessee State (Paul Hamilton) and Virginia Military Institute (Cal McCombs) all came from Fisher's staff. There's an even longer list of assistants who have moved on to top jobs. It's just an incredible mark Fisher has made on Division I-A football.

More than that, it is Fisher's character that makes the biggest impression. Come Sunday morning, you can find him at church regardless of whether he won or lost the day before. As the head of the Fellowship of Christian Athletes, I've often called on Fisher for various events and speaking engagements. He's never said no. He's been a tremendous teammate in every possible aspect.

Dal Shealy, President, Fellowship of Christian Athletes

"He wears me out"

My phone rang at 2 a.m. the day after Christmas, 1983.

"Coach. It's Fisher," the voice said. I recognized Fisher DeBerry's voice right away, despite the late hour.

"I know you like your job at the Citadel, but I've just been named head coach at the Air Force Academy," Fisher continued. "How would you like to come to Colorado Springs and coach?"

Ken Hatfield, who brought Fisher to the Academy, had left to coach at his alma mater, the University of Arkansas.

"Who left the staff?" I asked.

"Just about everyone's gone," Fisher said. "I'm the head coach now."

Fisher and I coached against each other when he was at Wofford and Appalachian State. When he was at Appalachian, we were in the same conference, so we recruited and played against each other. I got to know him real well during that time. I really respected him because of his enthusiasm and his faith.

I ended up joining Fisher's staff at the Academy. I considered it an honor to coach at one of the most prestigious schools in America. Knowing the kind of person and coach Fisher is, I knew it would be fun, though I wasn't sure how long I'd be out there. I told people two, three years at the most. I stayed 15 years and the fact that time passed so quickly says a lot about how enjoyable the experience was.

At the Academy, there was a collection of special people who really got the program going. Colonel John Clune, the athletic director, and Coach Hatfield really started the whole thing, as well as Fisher. Colonel Clune and the Superintendent of the Air Force Academy, General Winfield Scott, really saw the importance of having a good athletic program.

Fisher helped Coach Hatfield get the offense going, and then Fisher kept the program going during a critical time after it had first experienced real success.

The Academy already had been to two bowl games by the time I got there, so I view it as me just jumping on the bandwagon.

You look at all the success Fisher has experienced, and you quickly realize it is no coincidence that the other service academies started running the same offense that Fisher installed—or that one of his former assistant coaches, Charlie Weatherbie, is now the head coach at Navy.

I really don't think Fisher has gotten the credit he's deserved in helping the program get to such a high level. At the same time, Fisher is such a humble guy, he'd never accept the credit even if it were given to him. I mean, this is a coach who has won more football games than any other coach in Academy history. Yet if you saw him on the street or at the grocery store, he's just another guy.

Fisher is a person who has been blessed—and who really and truly knows he has been blessed. The Good Lord has given him a good mind and given him the opportunity to work with good young people. God has given him a platform—he coaches at a prestigious school and has a forum to positively influence young people.

I remember back in 1992, we were getting ready for a bowl game down the hill from the football offices on our practice field. One of our best players, Carlton McDonald, was stretching, and I was talking to him. We looked up and there was Fisher running down the hill at full speed. He had a hard time getting out of the office that day because there were so many preparations to make for the bowl. He wanted to make sure the players had a chance to have some fun and do some educational things while they were at the bowl.

Carlton looked at Coach DeBerry sprinting and shook his head.

"What?" I asked Carlton. "I hope you appreciate that man. He's been going over and beyond his responsibilities."

"I know," Carlton said. "I love him, but he has so much energy. He just wears me out!"

We both laughed. I could relate.

Those times were so good. I can't believe I got paid for what I did at the Air Force Academy. We enjoyed what we were doing and the people around us. Fisher put together a congenial staff that believed in what was going on at the Academy.

Fisher was my boss at the Academy, but whether we were coaching or mopping floors together, I'd still consider him my best friend. I'd go to work knowing he was my boss. But I always knew he was my friend and respected what I brought to the table.

Cal McCombs, head coach, Virginia Military Institute

"Call him 'Sparky' "

When Fisher became the head coach at the Air Force Academy in late 1983, he called me and asked me to join his staff. Ten days later, my wife, daughter and I packed up everything we had and moved out there on Jan. 9. Fisher took care of everything. He's more than a coach to me—we are very close.

Fisher knows a lot about football. But because of all the players he has coached, he sometimes forgets names. We were watching recruit films one year at the Academy. This kid was on the screen, and Fisher couldn't remember his name. He called him "Sparky" for the rest of the film. All of us assistant coaches were looking at each other like, "Who is 'Sparky'?" But that's Fisher. His heart is always in the right place, and he just makes you smile with his Fisher-isms.

Coach DeBerry and his amazing wife, Lu Ann, also turned us on to Hoppin John, a southern delicacy that includes black-eyed peas, sausage, green peppers and onions in a skillet.

Coach's faith makes an impression that lasts forever. We'd start our days with quiet time in the morning, keeping Christ in our lives and knowing everything fell under Him. One of the first churches Fisher and I went to in Colorado Springs was very small—not even 100 folks. Now, it's a good-sized church with more than 1,400 people. That was a good experience. I also appreciated the way Fisher approached faith in football. The team knew where he stood, but he never forced it upon anyone.

The Academy is such a good fit for Fisher and vice versa. You really see what the Academy stands for when you get back to the civilian colleges. Character is what the Academy is all about it—it epitomizes character. In a lot of ways, the academies are the last frontier in terms of discipline and building character. A lot of kids find plenty of wrong paths at civilian schools. It's just not that way at the Air Force Academy and that leads to success for the kids and the program. The bonds that are made are special. I still get calls today from guys who played for us at the Academy. I am elated to see how well they are doing.

Kenny Rucker, assistant coach, University of North Carolina

"Doing flips"

My evaluation of Fisher DeBerry comes from many standpoints, which is a good way to know a person.

As a football coach, he is truly outstanding. He's a great coach who takes the material that he has and wins with it. That's what Fisher has been able to do. He uses an offensive philosophy that many people don't think would work in a lot of places. But it fits them at the Air Force Academy. He's been very successful as a coach. He's a good tactician, and he's always let his assistant coaches coach.

He's also been good at surrounding himself with people of high moral character. That would be important anywhere, but is especially so at the Air Force Academy.

In our profession, he has been a leader, serving as President of the American Football Coaches Association, which was founded by Amos Alonzo Stagg and John W. Heisman, among others. Fisher is deeply respected in our profession and has been named National Coach of the Year, which is a tremendously high award. He's also served on many of our committees, including the ethics committee.

In 1996, the American Football Coaches Association celebrated our 75th anniversary, so our yearly meeting was a very special event that year. As the president, Fisher served as the emcee. There were more than 6,000 coaches in the room, and Fisher did a wonderful job. We had an entertainment program that was set up so at the end, this man in a costume—some kind of barnyard animal, I believe—did flips and somersaults all across the stage. This guy was really going at it. He disappeared behind the curtain.

Seconds later, he reappeared and took off his mask.

"Boy, that's got me wore out!" said Fisher DeBerry.

The house came down. Of course, it was set up to make it look like it was Fisher, though it wasn't. Still, I wonder how many coaches could have pulled the act off. Fisher's sense of humor and endearing southern drawl made him the perfect performer for that program.

I enjoy his friendship and fellowship.

From a moral standpoint, Fisher is a great leader. He always stands for the things that are right. He's been a tremendous asset to all the non-profit organizations that he supports. He's an excellent coach and more importantly, he's a good man. He's one of the most thoughtful people I've ever met. He's what this game really needs.

Grant Teaff, former head coach, Baylor, executive director of the American Football Coaches Association

"At his best facing adversity"

I had never met Fisher DeBerry before I was hired to coach linebackers at Air Force at the start of the 1984 season.

Fisher had hired Bruce Johnson to be his defensive coordinator. Bruce and I coached together at Marshall University.

While still on staff at Marshall, I returned home to Huntington, Virginia, one night late from a recruiting trip and got a call from Fisher. He asked me, "Do you want to be a Fighting Falcon?" And I accepted.

Fisher had made a few calls and based on Bruce's recommendation, added me to his coaching staff—I never even interviewed for the job.

A couple of days later I got my first glimpse of Colorado and the Air Force Academy. I visited Fisher, and he got to check out his new linebacker coach for the first time. I guess it was a leap of faith for both of us.

Fisher is an amazing person with many great qualities. I coached with him for 11 years and learned so many things before leaving the Academy after the 1994 season.

I feel that his best quality as a coach is his unwavering faith in people. His faith in God guides his personal life and that carries over to his family, players, coaches—and virtually everyone he has contact with. He always expects the best from everyone. I think that is why he gets everyone's best effort. People know he believes in them so they, in turn, try to justify that faith.

Fisher is at his very best when he is in adversity. Everyone knows about his tremendous football knowledge, motivational skills, recruiting abilities, etc. However, the thing most people don't realize is Fisher's toughness, especially when the chips are down. In 11 seasons, I never saw Fisher blame anyone for a loss. He would be critical of what "we" had done poorly and point out where "we" needed to improve, but he never pointed a finger. He never spent a moment crying about the past and was always fired up to get ready for the next game. Sometimes when we played poorly, he would have had every reason to explode and let off steam. But he would stay the course and get everyone focused on the job in front of us. He always demonstrated his faith in his coaches and his team. He never buckled under pressure. He truly believes the Falcons will find a way to win. That attitude of his is contagious.

I imagine some people will remember the wins, the bowl games, and so forth. But I carried away all the memories of the good times and the strength of Coach DeBerry in the tough times. He believed in us in every way. I always looked forward to coming to work. I knew that whether we won or lost, Fisher would never change. He would always support us and always have faith in us. I've never seen anyone enjoy winning more than Fisher or know a stronger person in defeat.

He keeps the faith.

Accordingly, so do the Falcons.

Jim Grobe, head coach, Ohio University

7

Your Biggest Opponent: Adversity

Adversity is part of the game and part of life. It is said that there are only two guarantees in life: death and taxes. Both of those involve adversity. Therefore, I guess it's safe to say that you can guarantee you'll face adversity in life, so add adversity to the list. Since you will face adversity, you have to anticipate it.

Every Saturday before our games, I tell our team, "There will be some adversity. I wish I could tell you what it will be. I don't know when or what it will be, but how you respond to it will speak volumes about the character of this team and how good we will be as a team. If you stick your head between your legs and say, 'Poor old me,' you won't reach the peak of your ability. However, you will if you say, 'Hey, this is part of it. We have to dig deeper and push harder. We have to come together a little stronger.' Then we CAN do it."

That's where your leadership kicks in on the field. You have to have your team as prepared as possible before adversity strikes. Surprises are not a good thing. That's where you get caught off-guard and that leaves you on your heels. It's not easy to push forward when you're leaning backward.

Still, "sudden change" will happen, but you can prepare for the possible scenarios in advance. The change could happen to us, with us fumbling on our own goal line. Or it could happen for us, with us getting the ball on our opponent's goal line.

If our offense fumbles it away on the one-yard line, what will the attitude of our defense be? Will the defense become angry and blame the offense or will they suck it up and say, "That's all right. No one's going to score on us. We'll get it back, offense; don't worry."

And how's our offense going to react? Are the players going to second-guess themselves and our play calling and get down on their brothers? Or are they going to keep their focus, draw on their discipline and go back out with a renewed commitment and desire? We pride ourselves on our reaction to "sudden change."

Accountability is the most important thing—again, that means not letting your brother down, being prepared and being at your best.

How you handle adversity is an attitude more than anything else because all the talent in the world won't keep you from fumbling at a given time. All the talent in the world won't overcome adversity if your attitude and character aren't right. That's why you see so many top-ranked teams tumble each year. Sure, it seems like a fluke when a team that's not even ranked beats a top 10 team, but what does it usually come to? Usually, it comes down to overcoming adversity. The favored team is faced with a situation it couldn't have predicted, and it doesn't respond in the right manner. That's why I respect the teams that have gone undefeated over the years. Those teams had adversity at key times against highly ranked teams or against unranked teams that were simply gunning for them—it makes a year complete for an unranked team to beat a highly ranked team. The lower team could go 1-10, but if it beat its chief rival while that rival is ranked, the season can be deemed somewhat of a success. Likewise, no one from the favored team will remember the wins if it goes 10-1—the team will remember the one that got away.

If you look at the few teams that have gone undefeated, they were led by remarkable coaches: Tom Osborne at Nebraska, Joe Paterno at Penn State and Bobby Bowden at Florida State.

Adversity has to be accepted as a challenge, not used as an excuse—at least that is how you aspire to see them respond.

We had a situation back in 1994. It was the year before Northwestern went to the Rose Bowl. We were facing them after we had lost our first two games, despite scoring 21 points in each. We dominated against Northwestern that whole day, but we fumbled on the two-yard line before the end of the first half. We still came back and had the lead. Then, with two minutes left in the game and us leading 10-7, we were on the Northwestern two-yard line. We ran the same play, with the same player, and we fumbled again. A Northwestern picked it up and went 98 yards for the winning touchdown to beat us, 14-10.

We were 0-3 despite playing great—outplaying our opponents. Our kids could have thrown in the towel right then and there, but the team came back to win eight out of nine games to finish 8-4. Our only loss as we went 8-1 over the final nine games, was a 42-30 defeat at Notre Dame, once again a game that we were in a position to win.

One of the big wins was the week before the Notre Dame game. We were hosting Utah after an emotional, hard-fought 10-6 win over Army the week before and a 34-17 win over Wyoming the week before that. We were playing well, but were getting beat, 33-14 at halftime.

We weren't playing badly, and I didn't rant or rave at the team. I just said, "Hey, Utah is playing well, but so are we."

We fumbled a couple of times, so it wasn't like Utah had stopped us. We had stopped ourselves. All we had to do was stop them and quit stopping ourselves. We went out in the second half and scored 26 unanswered points and won 40-33 in one of the greatest comebacks in NCAA history!

You have a lot of games and experiences like that, which are decided by attitude and character. I tell our team we won't lose any games—time might run out on us a time or two, but we will battle to the last second of every ball game. If we go down at the end, it won't be without a fight. We'll never give up!

At the same time, it's important to keep the kids at an even keel emotionally. I'd rather have 60 good minutes than 30 great minutes and 30 minutes of absolute shambles. We don't profane toward our players, and we don't put them down. Certainly, we'll point out what we need to improve on if we aren't playing as well as we need to. At Utah, it would have been easy to overturn a couple of lockers—of course, I was a few years younger then—but I can tell you that had I done that, we'd have lost the kids at that moment and then lost the game.

We had good dialogue and communication with the kids. We were able to keep the kids believing in themselves. That's the essence of coaching; When athletes reach a certain level of maturity—when the confidence is there to overcome adversity and the kids believe in themselves, their ability and they've put in the time—you should be able to bring them up to the highest level.

And you don't quit on each other. That's winning. So is this;

Winning

Winning is in the way you play the game each and every day
It's in your attitude and in the things you say
It's not in reaching wealth or fame

It's not in reaching goals that others seek to claim
Winning is having faith and giving confidence to a friend
It's never giving up or never giving in
It's in wanting something so badly that you could die
Then, if it doesn't come, be willing to give it one more try
Winning is being clean and sound of mind
It's being loyal to and serving all mankind
Winning is in your teammates, friends, family and what they
    learn from you
Winning is having character in everything you do
Winning…it's how you play the game

That puts it so well. Winning is about so much more than which lights are lit up on a scoreboard. Winning is about the game of life. You have to work to be a winner. It really doesn't come naturally or automatically.

That's why I constantly harp on: "You make the difference." I sincerely believe that has to be the attitude each of us takes every day. Everyone has responsibilities. The way you accept and execute that responsibility will determine ultimately how well you do your job, as well as how well the guy next to you does his job—and as a result, how the team does its job collectively. That's why we say, "Don't let your brother down" and "Do your job." If that happens, it's going to work because the way we have the system organized, everything is just about covered, and we will succeed if everyone does his job. You will be successful to a degree correlated directly to the "team" concept of your players and the commitment to "team first." If you have players committed only to their own statistics and glory, you will not be a good team. That's why big, talented teams fall year after year. You'll look at the NFL draft and see 12 kids taken from one college team, yet that team had three losses, including one to a school that had only one kid drafted or even none. Unselfishness has to be the cornerstone of your team.

That's why it's important to let everyone know as often as you can how appreciative you are of them doing their job and taking such pride and responsibility for it. There's a big focus on personal accountability at the Academy. It's also a big part of our football program as well.

8

The Value of Education

My grandmother always preached the benefits of education. She was a beautiful Christian lady. I am coaching because of my strong belief in education. She always said, "The teacher is probably more important than the preacher," because as a coach or teacher you have them at least five days a week, whereas the preacher gets them for only an hour or two on Sunday.

School is important for so many reasons. You learn, of course, but you also meet people.

Reading is the most basic of educational skills, yet it is the most important. If you are a good reader at a young age, your learning curve is much more manageable.

One of my regrets is that I'm not as well read as I'd like to be. I really like to read as many biographies of great people as possible. You can learn so much by reading what others have experienced. You take those lessons—good and bad—and you can apply them to your own life and share those lessons with others. The past few years especially, I've developed an even greater appreciation for reading.

I feel so incompetent when I walk into a bookstore. There's so much there that I don't know. Education teaches you to read and reading is a way for you to educate yourself. It's important more so today because society is changing.

There's so much information out there, especially with the increases in technology. The computer is still a foreign language to me in a lot of ways. But there's a great amount of knowledge you can learn via the computer.

Our younger coaches have experience on-line and can do a lot of things that really help the program. We get a lot of knowledge and preparation information on-line. You have to be proficient on the computer in this day and age.

It's ironic that all these technological geniuses have one thing in common—they are great readers.

I really respect the reading programs that have been instituted and promoted nation-wide. I really respect what reading advocates have done—President Bush's wife, Barbara, did some great things in that arena.

I take opportunities to read at elementary schools to let kids know how important it is and so do our players. If kids can see our players reading and showing how important it is, it does make an impression. Education promotes social opportunities as well. You can learn so much about people and your interests. You can learn practical things, like home improvement or any other hobby or interest you have.

One of my greatest experiences in school was in pre-school. We had a "little red schoolhouse" that was for pre-school, and my best friend's mother ran it. Even though we really didn't have the money for it, my mother scraped together the tuition to send me there, since it was a privately run venture.

We learned from the book, *All I Really Need to Know I Learned at Kindergarten.* It talked about how to take a nap and how to be respectful. When we finished that year, we had a graduation ceremony, and grandmama made me a little gown to wear.

Anything you do in life will involve reading. One of the key components to being successful in sports is reading.

9

For God . . .

Psalm 118:24—*This is the day the Lord has made; let us rejoice and be glad in it.*

I start a lot of my public speaking with this. I'll say, "This is the day (or night) the Lord has made." I like to share just a few of the things I'm rejoicing for. Sometimes, I'll start with how blessed I was to be brought up in a spiritual family or for the Fellowship of Christian Athletes or for my church and all the influence these organizations have had not only on my life, but how they fed my spiritual growth.

I'm glad and I rejoice everyday for all the great people in my life, those who have influenced me and helped shape me as a person.

In 1966, I went to the Sunday chapel that the New York Yankees had while they were on a road trip to play the Washington Senators. Many well-known major leaguers, including Bobby Richardson, Whitey Ford, Tony Kubek and Red Barber were there. Ol' Red was talking.

"This is the day the Lord has made; let us rejoice and be glad in it," Red recited.

"We should be grateful for every day and not ever take any day for granted," he told us. "We don't know the opportunities or challenges that we'll be presented with on any given day. But we should never forget to rejoice every day for our faith, our family and our health."

That is so true. All too often we get up and say, "Oh, God, it's morning!" instead of saying, "Good morning, God!"

The point Red was trying to make that day is that it's all a matter of attitude. There's a whole lot of people who either didn't make it out of bed this morning because their bodies wouldn't let them or people who have a lot more plight to deal with than the rest of us. Every day is a gift from God—time to spend with your family and friends, time to grow personally and spiritually and just another opportunity to make life better for someone you know—or maybe haven't even met yet. Don't view that opportunity as an obligation.

Matthew 5:16—*Let your light shine before men, that they may see your good deeds and praise your Father in heaven.*

To me, that word "light" means a lot of things—our work, our role model, our example to others, our influence, our responsibility and our walk as Christians.

We all have people we look up to now or have looked up to in the past. We have people whom we identify with or admire. Yet, we don't realize that there are some folks who are looking up to us. If you are a teacher, surely it is a student. Maybe it's a co-worker who sees qualities in you that he or she wants to copy. It might be your children looking up to you or a neighbor's kids.

As a coach at any level, you are put in a fish bowl, like it or not, simply because of the popularity of—and attention given to—sports.

That responsibility is as awesome as it is scary and exciting, especially when we consider that sometimes we don't even know when people are looking up to us. That's why it's so important to do the best job you can of constantly carrying yourself the right way, being responsible and caring, and not flying off the handle just because you're under pressure or having a bad day. What I'm saying here is that someone is looking at you most of the time and while we don't always realize that, it's still there. That's why the word "light" really stands out to me. Are you conscious and awake? Then your light is on and that addresses our influence.

Are you talking mean to your wife? The light is on. Are your kids listening? Are you bad-mouthing your neighbors around your kids? Are you stabbing someone in the back at work in front of others or even when you're alone with someone? The light is on. Is your light a shining example or is it a blinding glare? Don't forget about the light.

People say that "sticks and stones" break bones, but words don't hurt. Just the opposite is true. You don't remember scraping your knee in the second grade or falling off your bike in the sixth grade, but you probably remember your second- and fifth-grade teachers and particular things they said to you. Words stick around forever. Cuts heal up and scabs fall off, but words are internalized and taken to heart.

We all have a responsibility to our Christian walk. We have to be there for our brothers when they are in need. The Bible teaches us that we are our brother's keeper, so you have to be that light and be aware of it.

Philippians 4:13—*I can do everything through him who gives me strength.*

I sincerely believe this verse—it gives me a comfort to live. That doesn't mean I'm a superhero by any stretch of the imagination. You can't ask the Lord to deliver you miracle after miracle. By that, I mean that if you are bench pressing 250 pounds one day, you won't go home and pray to bench 400 pounds the next day and then come in and do it. Don't get me wrong, I subscribe to the miracles that occur when someone picks up a car to free a child or other superhuman feats of strength. We thank God for those miracles, but in day-to-day life, you have to do your homework, be prepared and be diligent. God's strength will guide you to where you are headed.

I think about Chad Hennings when I read this Scripture. Chad came to the Academy weighing 213 pounds as a freshman. He built himself into the greatest lineman in the country by his senior year. That earned him the Outland Trophy for the nation's best lineman. After earning his wings and flying attack aircraft for the Air Force, he now plays for the Dallas Cowboys.

The admiration and respect I have for Chad is immense. He is the same Chad today that he was when he was at the Academy. He signed a rather significant contract with Dallas, but success hasn't changed him at all.

He had a solid foundation in faith when he came here and he's held on to it. His mother and father gave him a tremendous work ethic on the farm where they raised their family. Chad also had foundations in other aspects that really helped him achieve. He knows God directed his path through his flight training and combat missions. Now he still wants to give God all the credit, and he wants to be the best father, husband and role model he can be.

We had another young man here in the early 1980s named Marty Louthan, whom I mentioned earlier. He has a great foundation of faith as well. When he came to the Academy, very few coaches around the country thought he'd be a Division I-A quarterback. But he was—and a great one at that. He ended up going back with us to his hometown to beat his hometown school, the University of Oregon. That's a classic example of this Scripture. Marty trusted God, worked hard and believed in himself. He gave all the glory to God because that's the foundation of Marty's life.

1 Samuel 2:30—*Those who honor me I will honor.*

I sincerely believe that God is trying to honor my life as I try my best to even feebly honor God. God appreciates people who try to do right. That is his promise to us.

That doesn't mean we always do right. I know I've made thousands of mistakes and used bad judgment or made poor decisions. Still, I always try to live for Him, and I know He will honor that.

I credit any small success that we have enjoyed in Falcon football to God. We have been steadfast in our commitment to give God all the glory, honor and credit.

Our church had 41 members in 1981 when it was first started. Today, we have more than 1,400 members, and I believe that incredible growth is from our commitment to honor God.

Mark 9:23—*Jesus said everything is possible for him who believes.*

Jesus is saying that if you believe, truly it can happen. However, you have to truly believe in your heart and soul— have faith.

If you believe, all things are possible. That's the attitude I have in our football program. If we take care of the things we can control, we can whip anybody. I believe all things are possible. I do truly believe in the power of God, that we can overcome anything. That means working hard, preparing well and believing in what you are doing.

1 John 2:6—*We profess our faith in God, then we must walk as Jesus walked.*

What a challenge that is—and it is an awesome task. That means to me that we ought to pattern our lives after the role model of Jesus' life.

John 3:16—*For God so loved the world that he gave his one and only son, that whoever believes in him shall not perish but have eternal life.*

Note the order of the words; love precedes giving. If you love, then you want to give.

This is kind of everybody's favorite Scripture. It is also probably one of the most well-known and referred to. There was an occasion when Dan Stavely, who coached at the University of Colorado, spoke to our team. He's an amazing man of God. One of the greatest tributes to a man I ever heard came from Brian Cabral, an assistant coach at the University of Colorado. On the night of Dan's retirement, Brian said, "I've never met or seen or heard of a man more Christ-like than Dan Stavely."

That is the ultimate compliment to anyone.

He has probably influenced more lives in this great state than most. Dan is a very good speaker. He often quotes from John 3:16 about how "God so loves that he gave"—and to me that is the priority and key to life. If you truly love those around you, you are giving without feeling like you have to give. You don't have to give in order to love. Rather, the message is that love precipitates everything, from giving of yourself to caring and offering help to those in need. Compassion comes from that love, from God.

Proverbs 3:5-6—*Trust in the Lord with all your heart and lean not on your own understanding; in all your ways acknowledge him, and he will make your paths straight.*

I think this is the Scripture that is the directional foundation of our program.

Along those lines, I have a saying on my desk that reads, "Nothing will happen today that the Lord and I can't handle together." This is a great theology and direction for anyone's life. If you put your trust in God and you know you'll find your way, then you will be on the right path.

Proverbs 16:3—*Commit to the Lord whatever you do, and your plans will succeed.*

If you trust your plans to God, your plans will succeed. You will find your way. We all have our paths, and I don't think we've done anything by ourselves. I don't pretend to have ever done anything all by myself. I'd like to think that I'm not that selfish or vain.

We've had outstanding players, assistant coaches and all other areas of personnel in this program. God has blessed some of our plans because we have tried to honor God and give him credit. We asked for His directive and guidance. For our program and team, a lot of our decisions are spirit led and I, of course, make no attempts to hide that. I'm proud that we have the Lord in our program as our Head Coach. He truly is the Master Coach of us all. God has been a great source of strength, guidance, perseverance and sustenance.

10

...And Country

The foundation of our football program at the United States Air Force Academy is family. We believe strongly in caring for your brother and not letting him down. That's why after every practice we grab each other's hand and we hug. We do that out of respect. While it is a game of competition—for spots on the depth chart and starting, as well as our offense against our defense—we are still one team. A lot of coaches I know of don't mind their players fighting in practice because it "shows fire" or the toughness of the team. We do not allow fighting here—ever. Fighting destroys the ideal of family, and we are all about family.

Think of it as paddling up a river, working hard to make headway against a current. Everyone in the boat pulls together to do that. Why would you waste energy in such an endeavor by being in conflict? Teamwork is about pulling on the same end of a rope. You can disagree without it leading to punches being thrown. In fact, differing points of view and varying personalities only add to a team concept. But when it's time for a tug of war, you all grab the same end of the rope. Fighting only destroys the bonds that you built through hard work. Trust, one of the truly overlooked keys to success in life and in personal relationships—which includes a team—is essential. You won't be trusting someone who took a swing at you in anger.

I believe the greatest gifts in life are—after my Christian faith—family and children. There is no bigger gift than a child and as a parent and coach, I realize there's no bigger responsibility than being entrusted by parents to have their child in my charge for four years here.

Being a coach, you are being entrusted with a family's most prized possession. That is both an awesome and scary responsibility, as well as a tremendous compliment. You have to treat the kids right. That means sometimes disciplining them or holding them accountable for something they did off the field. We have an equal responsibility to praise them for what they've done well and show them where they have room for improvement, as we do the responsibility to point out when they do something wrong and how to avoid repeating such a mistake again. When they fall short of accomplishing something, not only should we motivate them to reach the level they are shooting for, but to acknowledge the good things they did along the way, even though the net result isn't quite what it needs to be yet.

I don't take that responsibility lightly. I will provide love for that child, discipline and growth. I always expected my son, Joe, and my daughter, Michelle, to be embraced that way by their coaches. I hold myself to that standard year to year, month to month, day by day and minute to minute. Anything less would be unforgivable. I take pride in these kids' success and I know that if they don't succeed, I have let them down. So we are a family here and we always will be. The love of family can move mountains.

The kids here are ones who love to be successful—they have been successful, and they expect that from themselves. Our kids are highly motivated at the Academy. At the same time, they embrace challenge. So our staff gives them energy and direction.

We have a different motto every year, one that reflects our team, our goals and the way we are going to get there. Heading into the 2000 season, our motto was "Champions every day." We try to approach every day, one day at a time, one practice at a time and one game at a time. We realize if we do our best every play in practice, then we don't have to concern ourselves with who our opponent is. Our challenge is to ourselves—to play our best every play in each game. If that happens, we know that in the long run the ultimate goals of the season will take care of themselves.

We have the mottoes and provide the guidance because we have to help the kids find a direction and a route to get there—but make no mistake, they are the ones who go through the journey, with the staff there alongside providing direction and support.

We've had slogans such as No Limits, Raise the Level, Think Big, Take Care of Business and Expect to Win, just to name a few.

Before you begin any endeavor, you have to have a vision or a goal. You have to have a direction, and you have to have a way to keep that focus.

To that end, every year we give our players a decal to put on their watch crystal. That way, every time they look to see what time it is, they are reminded of their goal.

One year our slogan was "Whatever it takes." That doesn't just relate to doing whatever it takes to be champions and winning games and conference, but how you are living your life every day—what you are doing on the field as well as off the field. That means making a commitment to excellence in everything you do. You know that whatever it takes, we can do it, together.

We remind kids what has happened on the fields where we played. At Notre Dame in South Bend, Indiana, for example, we'll take them to spots on the field where great plays were made and tell them, "This is where you might make a big play tomorrow."

There has to be goal orientation in everything that you do or try to achieve. Every year I expect to be in the hunt for the conference championship—that's just a tradition and expectation we have. So we impress that upon our players. We show them how many young men went before them and gave all they had. That means the young men on this year's team are playing for their teammates as well as the players from the past who built this into a nationally established program and the ones who will follow this year's team long into the future. Each year, our kids have to live up to that tradition and standard. Then, they build on that tradition and make their own mark, which will set up the players who will follow them for success.

Our kids are first-rate, as is our program and entire staff— and that is by design. We have to do everything first class because that's what the American public expects from an Academy athletic team. We demand that our players represent the Academy in a first-class manner, from how they carry themselves to how they perform on the field. If we have eight turnovers and 100 yards in penalties on a Saturday, we aren't representing the Academy very well or serving the public interest the way we should. We must be, on the field and off, an organization that represents this country with pride, discipline and respect.

We have good athletes here. They might not be the so-called blue-chip athletes that a lot of the football powerhouses in the country tried to recruit. But they are kids who have a lot of pride and are self-motivated. They want to play football at the highest level. They realize the great opportunity educationally they get here. They have an opportunity for a career after they leave here, whether in the military or in the corporate world.

The biggest difference for the coaching staff here—and to me, this is a huge difference from the rest of the colleges—is that my coaching staff and I are here to serve the student-athletes, rather than having the kids serve us.

Often in college sports, a kid is signed to a scholarship and then his or her contribution athletically is the first and foremost obligation. But at the Academy, the obligation is to our country, the military, the classmates and the world. Academics do not take a backseat here. We don't "work to keep players eligible" by any stretch. Our student-athletes are standout students and while the challenges here are substantial, so are the resources to meet, achieve and exceed the standards set.

That being said, a player can achieve anything in football at the Academy that he can at another college. We've won conference championships, and we regularly play in bowl games. We've had a winning record in all but two years since I became head coach in 1984. We're usually battling for the conference championship, we've been in 10 bowl games and have been ranked among the top 10 in the nation. We've had players win, or be finalists for, the national individual awards that are given out annually.

Yet, we have never been listed among the top schools annually in recruiting. We don't get many high school All-Americans each year. That's just not going to happen for us. Still, our coaching staff knows that there are a lot of very, very good high school football players out there who want to play Division I-A football for a college that has a winning record and regularly goes to bowl games. So kids get that chance with us. They might be 40 pounds too light for a traditional football powerhouse, but we can address that here because we have a great developmental program. Our strength and conditioning program is one I'd put up against any in the nation. Kids come here wanting the opportunity to play Division I-A football. Once they get here, they will get anything and everything they earn. I've always said that the main reason we've been as good as we've been here is because our kids have embraced our off-season drills and lifting program. Our weight program, developed by Jack Braley and continued by the incredible staff of Allen Hedrick and Peter Melanson, does a great job year after year.

Lifting weights and conditioning serve another purpose for our kids—it's a good release for them from the academic and military aspects of their education. As I mentioned earlier, Chad Hennings, of the Dallas Cowboys, came here at 213 pounds. When he left here, he was the Outland Trophy winner as the nation's best lineman. When he graduated, he could have played anywhere in the country and been a star—but when he got here, he was another one of those kids who had the heart of a lion but the body of a cub. He worked so hard in the weight room—he's 300 pounds now, and left here at 275 pounds. Whenever I had to find Chad, I always knew where to find him—in the weight room.

Chris Gizzi was twice the conference Defensive Player of the Year and was of the same mold. Gizzi was also in the Denver Broncos camp. Steve Russ was one of our top linebackers and has played in the NFL, also with Denver.

For us, one of the greatest satisfactions as a coach is seeing a kid go from one level up to another and then another level. I love to see them do things that even they didn't think they could do. That being said, I don't think it takes a great coach to coach the great athletes. I think it takes great coaches to take players who aren't at that highest level and teach them and get them to believe in what they have to do—

with the ability they have—to improve and become a great team.

Certainly as a coach, you have to know what you are doing in X's and O's. But the intangibles have just as much to do with winning—relationships and trust are just as important in building a successful team and program.

We still have to emphasize being a smart and disciplined young man and player. One does not necessarily lead to the other, though it certainly can make it easier when you have those characteristics coming into it.

What I mean is this: I'm not sure there's a big correlation between being a great player and a smart kid, though I do think you have to be smart to be a great football player. Still, it's the "wanting to" as much as anything.

That carries over to the coaches as well. Coaching at an academy is different and unique. Certainly, it's not for every coach, as I'm not sure everyone is cut out to do it.

You have to coach here a year or two to learn the system. Football is not the only thing or the most important thing here. Players have a lot of other things grabbing their time and attention. That's what I appreciate about the cadet-athletes. They have to learn so much about time management and prioritizing everything they have to accomplish. They learn so many more lessons than what they get on the field, like how to put things in proper order and allocating certain amounts of time to get everything accomplished. They deny themselves a lot of social opportunities for the end result, a commission in the United States Air Force. It takes a lot of sacrifice to make it through the Academy. Playing Division I-A football requires even more sacrifice and commitment. Certainly there is sacrifice in any program. But here there is as much sacrifice as I've ever seen.

The important thing to remember is that you can achieve

anything here in football that you can achieve anywhere else. You can also get one of the most prestigious educations you will find anywhere in the country.

That's why it's so great for us to be able to coach kids who are inherently "winners." The quality of a person we get is important. These are young people of high moral character and integrity who have a great work ethic. If they aren't that kind of people, we won't ever see them because they won't make it through the screening process to get into the Air Force Academy. So as coaches, we look for young people who fit into the Academy's mission and academic standards. Sure, we lose a lot of potential cadets at that point. We lose others because they are looking for other opportunities. However, the ones we do get are truly gems, and we are fortunate to have that kind of person in our program—that is something we never forget and we never forget to appreciate and respect that, either.

I want the young men who enter this program to take a foundation with them that will help them in life. They come here as good kids, and I want them to leave here even better. I want them to be better prepared for the job they will have, for being a husband and father, and for serving their country—and representing their family—in the best, most honorable way possible. I want them to know what's right and to be prepared for the challenges they will face.

Having been in the military, I have a deep respect for the men and women who serve this country in uniform. I admire people who have given their careers and committed their lives to serving this great nation.

I always have respected the mission of the Air Force Academy, which is not to prepare professional football players but professional officers. I identified with that really well. Since 99.9 percent of all college football players on any given year are looking for a job outside of pro sports when they graduate, the Academy provides a unique opportunity for a great job in a great environment upon completion of the program here.

Whether or not the graduates stay in the military after fulfilling their commitment is somewhat of a moot point when it comes to future success. That's because the high-tech companies love to get Academy graduates when they leave the service. The Academy alums have all the skills and knowledge, drive and determination to join the high-tech world and step into a leadership role with major companies, often at age 27 or 28, if they choose to leave the service. Corporate America is always recruiting our officers when they've made the decision to enter the civilian world. Of course, if they stay in, their futures are also unlimited as career officers.

That's one of the real pluses coaching at the Academy. As a coach here, you get to be with some of the brightest and most talented young people in the country. It is certainly not hyperbole to say that we have some of the finest young people in America.

I often get asked why I didn't take coaching opportunities at other colleges. Since we've had a lot of success and played in a lot of bowl games, there certainly have been offers from other colleges.

One of the reasons I've stayed at the Academy is the kind of young person we are privileged to serve. Another reason is the unbelievable support we've received from the Academy itself.

What we are doing at the Academy is important. This is a leadership training school. And there is no better place to learn leadership than on the field of athletic competition— look down through the years and you'll see that some of the best military leaders were athletes as well. These former athletes have shown that they are good in time of conflict—

meaning they react well to pressure and make good decisions in that sort of trying, adverse environment.

What we are doing here with sports is important to the entire mission of the Academy. We don't go out and say, "Try real hard and maybe we'll win." We go out to win and to do that, we prepare to win every day in practice and in the weight room. We think it is important to win here because we want these kids to be warriors and winners. In a combat situation, there's no place for second place. You are competing for your life and the survival of your country and its ideals. We go out to win in a very, very serious way in every endeavor. We develop positive, winning attitudes. Saying, "We will have a winning record, and we will win the Commander-in-Chief's Trophy" is not a bunch of lip service trying to motivate kids. It's an honest goal—one that should we fail to achieve, we will take some hard looks at the points in our program that kept us from our goals. We know winning doesn't happen just on the field. It happens with every repetition in practice and every set of lifting in the gym.

You end up doing well at things you emphasize and focus on. We emphasize the little things because that is what leads to success in the big things. We take pride in the fact that we are going to be a disciplined team. The military system here at the Academy brings with it an innate system of discipline. While a lot of that is not directly related to football, there is a good spillover effect. We take pride in being the least penalized team in our conference. To our coaching staff, it is important not to take the easy way out—penalties can beat you faster than your opponent can.

There are four critical areas in football. The first one—and most critical—is the turnover game. That's a discipline issue—an attention-to-detail kind of thing. We know that if we win the turnover battle, we have a great chance of winning the overall war—which in this case is the football game. Just like anything in your career or your personal life, your own mistakes beat you quicker than anything else. So after every game, the first thing I look at is turnovers. In most instances, you look at the turnovers, and you can figure out who won the game by that statistic alone. Therefore, we emphasize taking care of the ball and work on that in practice. We have a punishment system for someone who can't take care of the ball.

The second important area is penalties. If you have fewer penalties, you have more total net yardage than the other team, which will give you another opportunity to have a better chance to win. That's also a discipline thing. We won't let someone keep jumping offsides again and again because it is too costly to the team and its goals.

The third important area is the kicking game. We've been pretty good at that in the 1990s. In fact, for the decade we were second to Virginia Tech in the number of kicks we blocked. That has won several games for us. We take a lot of pride in the kicking game—not just with talking about it either. We work very hard on it. We tell our players, "The highest compliment you can get is to be selected for our kicking team." That's why in our game program we publish the starting kicking teams, whereas most programs only publish starting offense and starting defense.

Our best players are on our kicking teams. The kicking game composes a third of the plays in the game. Think about how many times a kicking game play has determined the winner of a game. If you watch highlights, you'll see countless "game-winning field goals" or a "kickoff return that decided it" or "changed the momentum." Nothing changes momentum faster than the kicking game. It is often the most important play in determining the outcome of a game.

A fourth important part of the game is time of possession. In the possession game, you have to have the ball longer and run more plays than your opponent does. We believe the best defense we can have is to keep the other team's offense off the field. Therefore, we have a ball-control offense. We think it's important to run more plays than our opponents. If we've run more plays, then we've enhanced our chances of scoring more points—and just as important, we've limited the other team's opportunities to score. Our accepted norm here—our standard—is to score 30 points a game, run up 400 yards in total offense and run 10 to 15 more plays than our opponent. If that happens, then we're keeping our defense very fresh and thus, more effective.

We have a system like most coaches and ours on offense is the option. We have a moving, stemming, unpredictable and attacking defense. And we have to be solid in the kicking game. We will make plays in the kicking game. That is the foundation. You adjust from the foundation upward to the personnel you have. We graduate so many players every year because we don't have a redshirt system—something civilian colleges use that allows a player to sit out a year, usually their first year, and then still have four more years of eligibility. That gives them five years at the college. We have only four years at the Academy.

Therefore, unlike other schools, we aren't really able to make it so we graduate a certain number of offensive and defensive players and special teams players. It seems like one year it's a huge loss on the defense and the next year it's a big loss on offense. That's just the state of transition we face every year because of the lack of a redshirt year and our high academic and military standards.

As I have said, we get great kids here. It's a good system and one that they buy into and believe in. If we told them tomorrow that we were going to switch the option offense for a different system, the players probably would revolt. Our players believe so strongly in it, and our coaches have done such a good job of selling it to them that it would be out of the realm of consistency to shift systems in mid-flight and expect that trust to be there.

"Coach is going vertical"

We were playing at New Mexico, and it was right before halftime. One of our running backs, Greg Johnson, broke free down the sideline right in front of our bench. Coach DeBerry ran along the sideline, almost keeping up with Greg. As Greg ran toward the end zone, so did coach.

The only problem was that Coach still had on his headset. Around the 25-yard line, the cord for the headset ran out. Coach wore that headset so tight over his ears that when the cord ran out, his legs flew into the air. That's right: Coach DeBerry went vertical. Thank goodness, he wasn't hurt.

The next day, we were watching film of that game. When we got to that play, we must've watched it 40 times—not to watch Greg's run, but to see Coach DeBerry going vertical!

Film study was a big part of our routine. Like a lot of us, there would be times when Coach DeBerry would sneak in a little nap during the film, especially during one of his really long days. I'd see Coach asleep and since I, as a quarterback, knew a lot of defenses, would call out, "That's a monster middle." Well, Coach DeBerry would pop right up, "What monster middle? Run that back!" I honestly believe he could hear in his sleep.

The night before our games, we'd go see a movie. We'd usually do it on the road as well. We were in New Mexico for a big conference game and, Coach had it arranged so that we could get a theater downtown. Coach DeBerry wasn't really into movies. He'd just pick them from an ad in the paper or from what the clerk at the theater said when he'd call to reserve the theater.

The movie that night was "Child's Play." Coach thought it was a comedy, since it had a doll that talked in it.

Well, it wasn't. It was a horror movie that had this doll, "Chucky," that killed things and got killed. In fact, I think Chucky came back from the dead seven times. The look on Coach's face during the movie—when his face wasn't buried in his hands—told us that he was surprised by the content. The guys and I were laughing. What's Coach going to say tomorrow? Something like, "By Golly, everybody, I want you to come back like Chucky." Yeah, right, that would be perfect.

We went back to our hotel after the movie. The next morning, the atmosphere was very intense because this game was very important in our conference, as well as toward our post-season bowl prospects. We sat down at our pre-game meal, which was breakfast. Coach DeBerry could see we were way too tight.

"By golly, you guys," Coach DeBerry said as he stood up, "you saw Chucky come back last night. I want you to keep fighting and battling back like Chucky!"

We all fell over laughing. The tension was gone.

There's no doubt in my mind that "For God and Country" is a good title for this book.

However, I think "By golly" would have been more fitting!

I was a back-up quarterback to Dee Dowis, one of the top quarterbacks ever at the Academy and one of the best in the country while he was playing. While I was blessed to receive the Brian Bullard Memorial Award, I never did see a lot of game time because I played behind Dee. We were all watching film one night in South Bend, Indiana, before playing Notre Dame. I was sitting next to Dee Dowis and Assistant Coach Charlie Weatherbie. Coach DeBerry likes to ask us questions during films. After one play, Coach DeBerry asked, "Lance, when you see that defense tomorrow, what are you going to do?" I said, "If I see that defense, I'm throwing the bomb." He said, "You do that, and you're sitting next to me." So I quipped, "What, am I starting tomorrow?" Everyone laughed, even Coach DeBerry.

To the coaches and our trainer, the late Mr. Jim Conboy, it was important that we have prime rib the night before the game. We were in Utah for a big game and the restaurant didn't have prime rib. They kind of passed off this really raw steak as prime rib. Everyone's plate was full of blood. They were either just taken out of the freezer and thawed, or they were cooked for less than a minute.

Coach DeBerry was trying to put his best face on as he ate, as though he was trying to convince himself that it was okay. Every time someone would cut a bite, a vein would get cut and blood would spurt. Finally, Coach DeBerry walked around asking the players if their steaks were all right. We ended up sending back quite a few of them. But Coach did his best to work through it until he saw that none of us was enjoying it, either.

We had a lot of big games during my career at the Academy. We always knew how big a game Coach viewed it as during our final practice of the week before the game. We'd all "take a knee" and listen to Coach go over things with us after that final practice. We measured the importance of the game by how many times we had to switch knees during his speech. When it was a "26-knee" changing speech, it was a pretty big game and a lot was on the line. When it was only a five- or six-knee-er, then we were in pretty good shape and, we should roll if we did our jobs.

Coach DeBerry gave us a lot of smiles, but the most important thing is what he gave us as young men. He cared about us so much. Any guy who played for Coach DeBerry will tell you that the most enduring memory is what he'd tell us after every game. "Go to church tomorrow, call your mama and daddy and tell them you love them and remember who you are." I'll never forget that. I think everyone remembers that.

That's the one thing I liked the most about Coach DeBerry. He always kept God first. I don't know that we all did all of those things every time after each game, but it was still good advice. And as you hear it again and again, it makes an impression on you—the best kind of impression about what's important and what matters, who got you where you are and who you are as a person.

He gives all the seniors a Bible after their football career concludes. He wrote that "remember who you are" in the front of my Bible. Of course, since I have kids now, I'll tell them the same things as they get older—especially the part about calling their parents!

I stopped by Coach DeBerry's office while I was in Colorado Springs during the Christmas break of 1999. He was there alone and was generous enough to spend an hour with me, asking about my family and how things were going for me. The fact that he's so interested in his players as people says the most. That's why it's all about brothers and family in Falcon Football.

Lance McDowell, Class of 1990

"No Luck for the Irish"

I never will forget watching Air Force and Notre Dame play in South Bend, Indiana, in 1983. I was a freshman that year and a junior varsity player. But the game reinforced all of the reasons that I had chosen to attend the Air Force Academy. Coach DeBerry was the one who recruited me in 1982 and made a statement that I remember well: "We will play as hard on the last play of the game as we do on the first, no matter what the scoreboard reads."

I wanted to be a part of that kind of program and play for a coach who thought that way. With only one second left on the clock as we played Notre Dame, the Irish lined up for a field goal that, if made, would give them the win. As the ball was snapped, Chris Funk, our defensive tackle, was able to find a way to get his hand in the air and block the kick. That saved our victory. Although I didn't play in that game, I consider it one of the greatest moments in Air Force football history. Every young man who has ever played football is familiar with the mystique and tradition that Notre Dame football has possessed through the decades and the many great players and coaches who have won National Championships there.

Only one year later, in 1984, Air Force was back in South Bend to attempt a highly improbable feat: Beating Notre Dame for the third year in a row. Notre Dame was big and fast and well-coached. At Air Force, we had lost a great group of seniors from the previous year's team. There was no doubt that the odds were stacked against us to begin with—after all, this was Notre Dame. Factor in that we were very young and inexperienced and it seemed like we could be counted out—and we were by the "experts."

During our Friday practice at the stadium in South Bend—yes, we did play there two years in a row instead of rotating back to the Academy in 1984—Coach DeBerry blew his whistle and gathered the team for a few words. We all knelt as he began by saying, "Many great players have played here, right where you are kneeling."

I thought about it and how right he was. All of us were ready to hear Coach DeBerry rattle off names from Knute Rockne to Joe Montana. But Coach DeBerry wasn't thinking that way. "Yes, many great players have played on this field, and I just want to list a few of them: Marty Louthan, John Kershner, Mike Kirby, Chris Funk..." As he read the list of the prior year's Falcon seniors, we all smiled. Those were great players, and they did play on this field—and we knew at that point that we belonged there too. We were focused on the job at hand and won the next day by two touchdowns.

Coach DeBerry recruited me, coached me and allowed me to coach on his staff. I've often marveled at his ability to build and sustain a program that consistently competes on a national level, maintain relationships with hundreds of former players, remember birthdays, send cards to parents, visit people in the hospital and surround himself with some of the finest assistant coaches in college football. He is a devoted husband and father. He always has time to chat with everyone he meets, regardless of the stature. He's always quick to give credit to others and, first and foremost, to Jesus Christ.

Only two years ago, Coach DeBerry flew into Mississippi to support the Fellowship of Christian Athletes ministry. My wife, Aimee, and I picked him up. We were driving him to the dinner where he would be the guest speaker. He asked about my parents, Bubba and Sheila. I told him that Bubba was in the hospital with a serious heart condition. Despite the fact that we were on a very tight schedule and that he had traveled all day during a very busy stretch in his schedule, he told me, "Take me to the hospital right away. I have to see your dad." We went to the hospital, and Coach DeBerry brought a great deal of encouragement to my parents during a very difficult

time. My parents have told me often that any parent should jump at the chance to have their son play for Coach DeBerry. I'm sure glad—and grateful—that I had that chance.
Pat Evans, Class of 1984

"A young man's gift: Enthusiasm"

When I first met Coach DeBerry as a young freshman at the Air Force Academy in 1980, I knew he was a man with a mission. There was no neutral ground. His enthusiasm bubbled over. As is customary, we exchanged handshakes. If you ever shake his hand, you remember it. No one shakes more vigorously, firmly or intently. I remember him asking us freshman quarterbacks, "What quality is most important for a man to possess?"

His answer? Enthusiasm!

This happened 20 years ago, and I remember it like yesterday. You see, he was teaching more than football. He was training young men to be men.

In many ways I consider myself fortunate to have spent four years with Coach DeBerry as my QB coach. These were the years just prior to his reign as head coach. He is and was a consummate worker. Always focused, preparing, planning. He coached not only the quarterbacks for four years, but also the fullbacks. If that wasn't enough, the last three years he served as the offensive coordinator. This he accomplished with exuberant enthusiasm, never showing us the stress and all the hard sacrifices behind the scenes.

I once remember wondering aloud to his wonderful wife, Lu Ann: "Why does he continue to push us so hard?" She graciously gave me some insight into his motivation. He wanted us to reach our full potential. He wanted to leave no stone unturned in the quest of having us reach our very best.

He gave his all for us—these 20-year-olds whose performance on the football field on Saturdays would secure his job another year. Yes, I am sure he was concerned about his job with a wife and two kids at home. But he never let on this concern. Coach is competitive and has a love for the game. Not many jobs are as hard as coaching college football. Long days, seven days a week during the season, endless hours watching film of your own team and other teams. They start early (5-6 a.m.) and finish late (8-11 p.m.). The sacrifice is daunting, and thus the thrill of victory almost overwhelming, for both players and coaches. To work this hard makes defeat unbearable. The stakes are high and few are as successful as Coach DeBerry. As the coaches would tell us, though, for every hundred men who can handle adversity, only one can handle success.

Marty Louthan, Class of 1984

"Brothers are hard to beat"

He stood there addressing us for nearly an hour the first time—180 shaved heads knowing little about him and less of what he would teach us about ourselves.

He knew.

He was holding two pencils in his hand. He was to show us that alone he could break the pencil easily, but if he tried to break the two together, they would not yield. He told us of his growing up in South Carolina about these two brothers who were unstoppable on a basketball court because they knew each other so well.

The snickering was restrained as Coach couldn't get that first pencil to break. You could tell he was struggling to make one of the true core points of his philosophy on this first day of addressing his new freshmen, and he couldn't get that darn pencil to break. With two hands he finally snapped it, then showed he couldn't do it with two pencils. "Brothers are hard to beat!" he repeated. Man, we used to tease him about that.

We understood so little of his message that day. Fortunately, as those of us who played and coached for him know, Coach DeBerry is not afraid to repeat himself.

Four years later, 20 or so of those shaved heads were left; the senior core of a team about to play Ohio State as the biggest underdog in Liberty Bowl history. We had been through basic training, SERE (Survival, Evasion, Resistance and Escape training) and four years of academy life together, many challenges that most college football teams never see. We had learned to depend on each other, having to win our final three games to even be bowl eligible. This included a win in a rainstorm at Army, which hadn't been done in years. We had no Dee Dowis or Chad Hennings on this year's team, and the games we won seemed to come from different places each time.

Ohio State had missed going to the Rose Bowl by the narrowest of margins, and it was clear that Ohio State shouldn't have even been in Memphis, Tennessee. It was equally clear that we shouldn't have been there either. They outmatched us in almost every category, especially in the number of future draft picks, but I'm not sure they had ever seen their coach struggle to break a pencil or learned how hard it is to break many pencils standing together.

That night was the essence of what Fisher DeBerry brings as a coach. We dominated that more talented team. And although we had some great individual performances by guys like Brian Hill and Rob Perez, they will be the first to tell you that that game was won by a philosophy. We won by losing ourselves in our teammates.

I remember watching the final seconds tick off that clock. I was surprised that I didn't feel the ecstasy or redemption of beating one of the great programs in college football history—that would come later. I had one of those rare moments of clarity where one truly appreciates the gravity of life's lessons learned. I was prouder of us than I have ever been of me.

I think that was the moment that I realized Coach DeBerry's greatest gift. He somehow teaches that your proudest moment comes when "me" gives way to "we."

Understanding the depth of this gift requires consideration of what kind of kid comes to the Air Force Academy. These are all hyper-achievers who have been successful by distinguishing themselves above others. These are kids who already have learned that you rely on yourself and make your own way. Something like 25,000 applications get to the Academy every year. Around 1,300 get in and about 950 graduate. Obviously, this is a group who has a head start on understanding personal achievement.

If you aren't clear about that on arrival, this idea becomes clear to you early and often. Your performance will determine how soon you can own a car, how many weekends you may get to leave campus, whether or not you will fly and what type of plane, etc. etc. etc. I don't mean to knock this philosophy as it is a proven leadership model, and I wouldn't want our academies to recruit kids who think that a tie is a fine way to end a game or a war. But taking this type of kid, in this type of environment and getting him to believe that sacrificing every personal goal for the success of his teammate, will make him infinitely prouder of himself than any personal honor ever could—now that's a gift. And this is how the giants are slain.

J.T. Tokish, Class of 1991

"Call your Mama"

Coach DeBerry is a man whom I have held in high regard for many years. Though there are many ways that he has influenced my life, the one moment I will never forget was the conclusion to the post-game speech after every game, win or lose. Coach DeBerry would stand in front of us and talk to us about how we did in the contest. Then he always would end with three directives to us.

He always would say, and I quote, "Tomorrow is the Lord's day. I want to see every one of you go to church and thank the Lord for what He has done for you. After that, call your Mama and tell her that you love her and how important she is to you and finally, remember who you are; never do anything to blacken the eye or dampen the image of your family and the Air Force Falcons."

Without coming out and stating his priorities to us,they were evident in Coach DeBerry's life. This post-game speech has been replayed many times in the minds of his players. Long after the game was over, Coach stressed what was really important in life. As you see, he is not only a teacher of football, he is a teacher of life.

Coach always was quick to stress the importance of God and family to all his players. Whether it was talking about his 90-year-old grandma, who could have made that tackle, or speaking of the Falcon family, Coach DeBerry always let us know what was important in his life and what was important in the lives of his players.

This was never more evident than in the fall of '90. It was

the Tuesday of Army week, a pivotal point in accomplishing one of our primary goals; win the Commander-in-Chief's Trophy. I was a senior, a master LB at defending the Wishbone, and I was ready for the challenge. That was until I got a phone call. My father had had a heart attack and was in intensive care in Ohio. Without another care in the world, I raced home to my father's side. No other thought had ever crossed my mind but getting to my Dad, the coach who had taught me everything I had ever known.

When I reached the hospital, the nurse handed me a note. It was from Coach DeBerry and all of my Brothers (teammates, but we referred to each other as brothers from the day we showed up), offering their prayers and hopes for my dad. With all of the hopes and prayers of my entire family, in Ohio and in Colorado, my father quickly was released from the intensive care unit, but was still not out of the woods.

Coach DeBerry personally called every day to check on my father. Even though he was a very busy man and facing a formable opponent, he still was concerned about his extended family. On Friday, Coach DeBerry called and offered to fly me to West Point, New York, so that I might participate in the game against Army. This was my senior year and the last time I would face Army. I believe that he called not because he needed me, rather he thought I needed the Falcons to get through this. He also offered to fly me back to Ohio after the game to be back with my father.

Although I was very committed to the game, my father's health was the most important thing in my life. I very courteously declined and Coach DeBerry understood. Thank God, my father quickly recovered and on the next Wednesday, I returned to the Academy and to my brothers who so diligently had prayed for my family through this crisis. I was welcomed back formally by Coach DeBerry and then presented the game ball from the Army game that was signed by all of my "Brothers." This is a treasure that will be with me the rest of my life. Although this is only a football, it is a symbol of the support and love of all of my "Brothers."

Everyone knows that Coach Fisher DeBerry is a great

football coach. That is merely a part of this man. He is a great man and I admire him greatly.

Bill Price, Class of '91

"The name escapes me"

When the opportunity to reflect memorable stories about Coach DeBerry presents itself, anyone who has had the chance to spend six minutes with him, let alone six years as I have, could fill volumes. I entered the program in 1987 as a freshman walk-on, a nameless face among 120 cadet athletes in my class. Coach DeBerry was one of the first people I recall addressing our group. He emphasized giving each player, recruited or walk-on, the opportunity to prove himself and make a contribution to the proud tradition that is Falcon Football. I left four years later as a three-year starter, who helped the "Birds" achieve one of the most improbable wins in school history, thus securing a place in Falcon Football history for my class.

Along the way there were many memorable moments, some light-hearted, some not, that make Coach DeBerry a man I admire for his leadership and savvy on the gridiron, but more for his compassion, integrity, and enthusiasm off it.

The Academy never failed to do anything first-class, and Coach DeBerry was instrumental in ensuring that the highest standards were upheld when we traveled for away games. One of the most memorable road rituals was the Friday night movie at a local theater whenever possible. It was amazing that Coach never had a problem taking 65-70 19- or 20-year-olds to a local theater to catch a flick.

I knew we were big boys and always would carry ourselves as gentlemen, but taking a big group out on the town was not without risk. I sometimes thought that Coach D worried about the potential for child's play and wondered what he did to ease his mind during those nights in the theaters. I realized why Coach D was never going to be bothered by our actions in the theater when I walked up the aisle to take a bathroom break and happened to walk by his seat. It seems Coach D used the movie nights to catch up on lost sleep throughout the week! He could recall the movie endings in great detail, but never too much about the circumstances leading to them, and that night I learned why!

One of Coach D's most legendary stories revolves around his ability or lack thereof, to remember names. Before the 1989 Army game at the Air Force Academy, the Secretary of the Air Force (Dr. Ball I believe was his name) paid our team a visit at dinner on Friday evening to wish us the best on the field on Saturday. The Secretary was all smiles as Coach D stood to present him for his remarks.

It goes without saying that the Secretary of the Air Force has many opportunities to speak to crowds more esteemed and dignified than a football team, but he sure seemed caught up in the buzz and fervor of the anticipation on the eve of Air Force vs. Army. Coach D did nothing to quell his excitement.

"Guys, it is an honor for me to present your number one fan, the man who touts your exploits every week in our nation's capital to the most powerful military members in the country. Please welcome Secretary uh, er, hmmm, well, uh, Secretary…" As the smile left Secretary Ball's face and he patiently whispered his name in Coach's ear, I figured our exploits on the field would not be the only hot topic for discussion in D.C. the next week!

Coach D has never lacked an ability to provide humorous tales that provide all who played for him countless moments of light-hearted fun, but his mark as a football coach and most importantly as a man, has been made in a much more serious vein. The anecdotes, quotes and phrases that marked his pre-game and post-game talks and end of practice speeches are with me today. "This is the day the Lord has made, let's rejoice and be glad in it," "There are no shortcuts to success," and one I will never forget, "Brothers are hard to beat" will forever be sources of inspiration. Any man who maintains a steady walk with the Lord, no matter what his field of endeavor is one to be admired. A man whose love for the Lord and enthusiasm for life and the people in it helps to lead others to a more steady, focused walk with Christ years after their encounters with him may be called a saint, or simply, Head Football Coach at the United States Air Force Academy.

Brian A. Hill, Class of 1991

"Because it's all about family"

When I went to my first day of football practice during Basic Cadet Training, I saw that I was listed sixth out of eight strong-side inside linebackers on the depth chart. As everyone associated with the program knows, the coaching staff recruits over 100 freshmen players every year with the hope that at least 20 percent will develop into outstanding players by their senior year. Along these lines, the linebackers were listed as strong and weak side, so the coaches really needed to fill two positions. Effectively, this meant, on my first day of college football practice, I was listed as either 12th or 13th out of the 16 potential inside linebackers. I preferred to think I was 12th because I was listed on the strong side—ha-ha.

By the Blue-Silver Game, I had worked my way up to second team as a strong-side inside backer and was getting a lot of reps with the first team. While playing inside linebacker with my freshman roommate, Vergil Simpson (he was moved to outside linebacker later during his freshman year and after his senior season was named to the all-time USAFA team), we were nicknamed "Salt and Pepper." During the Blue-Silver Game, I was on a blitz up the middle and dove to make the tackle while chasing the option. When I landed on the Astro-turf, I separated my shoulder, chipped a bone, and tore some ligaments. I would require arthroscopic surgery the next week and wound up missing the entire season.

The day after my surgery, Coach DeBerry and his wife came to visit me and stayed for about an hour. Although I was fortunate enough to spend Doolie Day Out at Coach's house, I'm sure that we hadn't formed a special bond in those two hours. I was equally sure that he wasn't counting on me as a major contributor to the team that year. Really, I was just another of the 100 or so freshmen who was trying to move up the depth chart. It wasn't like I was a big loss for the program that year. Still, Coach DeBerry genuinely cared for me and my well being. He took the time out of his busy schedule to drag his wife to the hospital and check on one of his 16 freshman linebackers. The next day his wife again came by. She brought me cookies and spent about another 30 minutes. While I'd listened to Coach DeBerry's sermons about the importance of thinking of the team as our family for only three or four weeks, I got my first taste of what he meant while I was in the hospital.

Throughout the season, Coach DeBerry would check on me and ask how my rehab was coming along. After participating in the grueling "cage" sessions in the off-season, I entered spring practice with what I thought was a completely healed shoulder. That spring, I worked my way up the depth chart again. Going into the Spring Game, I was listed as the second-string strong-side backer for the Silver squad. During the game I was hit underneath the shoulder pad and dislocated the same shoulder. This time, I would require reconstructive shoulder surgery and was out eight months—my entire sophomore season!

At this point it would have been very easy for the coaching staff to write me off with the dreaded "injury-prone" label and forget about me. If I were strong-minded enough to stick with the rehab and physically able to compete again, maybe I would be able to contribute to the program. If so, it would be a bonus. Otherwise, no big deal. Shockingly, this was not the response I received!

Again, Coach DeBerry stopped by to visit me in the hospital. Only this time, the next day, my position coach and his wife showed up. By this time I had heard all about how tough it was to whip two brothers in a fight and had come to appreciate the meaning of viewing your teammates as family. However, to get this treatment from Coach DeBerry and his staff truly was special. I had friends playing ball at several football powerhouses who confirmed that the support I was receiving from the coaching staff was definitely not what they'd experienced. Typically, this type of treatment is reserved for senior starters or all-conference performers. Yet, here I was just battling for some varsity playing time, and Coach DeBerry was treating me like a real member of his family.

After going through extensive rehabilitation and strength training, I was again ready for the rigorous "cage" off-season training program and entered spring ball with a healthy shoulder. I made it through the spring session without injury and earned the second-string varsity strong-side inside linebacker spot.

As fall practice unfolded, I was caught in the "numbers game" and told that due to the history of my shoulder, the coaching staff had decided to give a sophomore the reps at second string. From a team perspective, I clearly understood the logic, but from a personal perspective, after working so hard to get back healthy and prove my value to the team, I was hurt by this demotion.

Rather than begin my junior campaign on the JV, I decided to leave the team and play baseball. I met with Coach DeBerry and my position coach, Jim Grobe, and informed them of my decision. They were both very understanding and genuinely showed concern for the health of my shoulder. Not only were they both looking out for the best interests of the team, but also they were looking out for the long-term health of one of their family members. Both stated that they would hate for me not to be able to throw a ball with my children someday. I thought about this and agreed that I was making the right decision.

As it turns out, I wound up dislocating my shoulder several more times over the course of the next year and half doing a variety of activities. I required a second reconstructive surgery after graduation and have since had to curtail my athletic participation. I am, however, able to throw a ball and look forward to throwing one to someone in my family one day.

Pat Hopper, Class of 1993

"Making his point at The Point"

Quite often we attempt to conjure thoughts of people who have been influential or made a difference in our lives. We often conclude that those persons are ones who helped us succeed in our quests, attain our goals, motivate us towards our pursuits, lift us when we are down, and humor us to raise our spirits. Fisher DeBerry was and is all those people rolled up into one very special person.

My connection with Coach DeBerry is simple. I'm one of the thousands of young cadets whom he has led to success. You see I was a quintessential Air Force offensive lineman. Every odd was stacked against me. I was small (6 foot and 235 pounds), slow, injured, weak, and enamored with an Eastern North Carolina twang that left me an extremely large hill to overcome. With all those qualities in my favor (trust me, I enjoy challenges), I wanted to play Division I-A football.

In high school, I excelled to the greatest extent possible and felt I had a chance to play football at an NCAA Division III school or, with a lot of luck, maybe a service academy. Regardless, the Naval Academy said I was too small. Army seemed disinterested and my only chance was with Air Force.

I remember being invited to the Air Force-Army game at West Point in 1990 as a guest of the Army football program. As a side note, I wasn't very impressed with Army's program and hospitality. So, given the fact that I was interested in the Air Force Academy, and my dad, Doug Thurston, knew Coach D from their days together at Wofford College, I eagerly sought to speak with Coach D at the first available opportunity. It was raining buckets that day and during warm-ups, as I watched Coach Noblitt drill his offensive lineman, Coach DeBerry recognized my dad and immediately rushed over to introduce himself. With no recourse, I told him I was on a visitation to Army, and Coach D's first instinct was to invite me into the Air Force locker room immediately after the game. I didn't even attend the post-game events for Army recruits. From that day forward, my time was dedicated to Air Force football. I'll never forget that day! Coach D made me feel like a part of the team.

From that day on, Coach D didn't have to recruit me anymore. I was sold. I venture to say hundreds of other recruits have had similar experiences with Coach D. You see his demeanor and amiable attitude always wins over his audience. There are countless events that I can remember—the 1992 Liberty Bowl, the Annual Children's Christmas Charity, the 1995 Copper Bowl, church events, and speeches at local athletic clubs—where Coach D's verbosity made him the center of attraction.

At times, he was too garrulous. For a man with such intellect, it's sometimes difficult, I'm sure, to keep an "after practice" speech under a few minutes. His hubris would force him to go on and on, jumping from topic to topic, with every intention of conveying the meaning of his tirade, but failing to see the connection between each point. For instance, who in the world, other that Coach D, can put together a sentence like: "There's nothing I hate more than not converting the center/quarterback exchange, so by golly, call your mama and get your E.I.!" (Extra instruction is an academy term used for getting additional instruction in challenging classes.)

Of course, everyone understood his intentions, but I don't think anyone could say it in that good ol' Cheraw, South Carolina, accent.

On a similar note, his upbringing in the bayous of South Carolina, taught him some colloquialisms that pertain to our everyday lives. For example, Coach D would say, "If you see a turtle on a fence post, you know he didn't get there by himself!" As a cadet, one fails to see the meaning behind such wisdom. But now, looking back, that quote exudes the values of teamwork.

There is no doubt in anyone's mind that Coach D. is a man whose didactic speeches scream with enthusiasm. He could make an "elephant walk a tight rope" if he wanted to.

Has anyone ever asked why Fisher DeBerry does what he does and why he is so successful? The answer is because, first and foremost, he understands the value of surrounding himself with good people. If you ask any person who has ever played at Air Force about their experience, they will rave on and on about their position coach. I know I owe everything to Coach Bob Noblitt. The true testimony is that Bob Noblitt, Cal McCombs, Paul Hamilton, Charlie Weatherbie, Richard Bell, Dick Enga, Chuck Peterson, Tom Miller and all those that have proceeded or come after, are all highly sought and well respected in the coaching community. Coach D was instrumental in their success, and likewise, Coach D is successful because of them.

The bottom line is that Coach DeBerry really cares about his family, friends, coaches and players. He is a dynamic Christian who places morals and values number one, no matter what the cost. If you ask any of the 20 or so seniors that walked the walk for four years, they will attest that Air Force football gave them the passageway and set them down the right path to succeed in life. Coach DeBerry had a more than significant part in that process. He is honored and respected by all those who have encountered him. I value my relationship with Coach D. I am thankful that he walked up to me that memorable day at West Point in 1990.

Rocky Thurston, Class of 1995

"A promise kept"

I answered the door and saw a short, sort of balding gentleman with the southernmost of southern accents. He was accompanied by two familiar faces, Charlie Weatherbie and Ken Rucker. These two men were assistant coaches to the man with the accent, Fisher DeBerry, head coach at the Air Force Academy.

Having just returned from visits to the U.S. Naval Academy at Annapolis and the U.S. Military at West Point, it was time for me to hear what the Air Force Academy had to offer.

Unlike many others in my "recruiting class," I did not have to be sold on the idea of either joining the military or attending a service academy: I had wanted to do so since I was 13 years old. But much to Coach DeBerry's chagrin, it was the military itself that piqued my interest rather than the Air Force Academy in particular.

Coach Weatherbie laid the groundwork late my junior year of high school with talk of flying jets and the grass surface rather than Astroturf at the other academies' stadiums. Air Force also had an impressive win-loss record against Army and Navy. Still, I remained dead set on attending West Point and serving in the Army as my father had done in Vietnam as a young officer.

Our high school had an exceptional season my senior year. We were 14-2 and Texas state champions in 5A ball (no need to call it "football" because only one type of ball matters in Texas, at least during fall). My personal stats weren't bad either, so all three academies were recruiting me. The first trip I took was to Navy. I went with the quarterback and fullback from my high school team and almost convinced myself to be a Marine while I was at Annapolis. A week later, I went to see "high school on the Hudson"—the U.S. Military Academy at West Point—where I quickly conjured up images of playing four years of football at "The Point" and living their motto of "Duty, honor, country."

It was not long afterward, upon returning home, that Coach DeBerry arrived at my house. Always the gentleman, he told my parents of his enduring love for Air Force and Falcon football. His comments on the Air Force Academy's prowess in the Commander-in-Chief's Trophy competition were equally impressive and backed by thoughtful comments from the assistant coaches at Air Force who had been recruiting me.

But it was a promise Coach DeBerry made that day that cinched my decision. It was late in the day and DeBerry sat with my parents and me.

"And by golly, Chris Howard," Coach DeBerry said, "if you come to the Air Force Academy and play for me, I promise that..."

In that split second, I flashed back to the year before in the same room. My brother, Reggie, was being recruited by none other than University of Oklahoma coach Barry Switzer. I listened enraptured as Switzer promised my brother a lot of things, including to expect All-American honors, trips to numerous bowl games, and a good shot at playing in the NFL. So as I remembered coach Switzer's lofty promises, I listened intently as Coach DeBerry started to make his promise. What would he promise me? A starting position? How about 8-0 vs. Army and Navy? A trip to the Holiday Bowl? In that short moment, a dozen scenarios popped through my head.

Coach DeBerry said: "I promise that...I will work your tail off!"

And with that, I knew I had to be an Air Force Falcon and play for this man. I've known him a decade now. The guidance, opportunities and support he's provided for me made the decision one I will forever cherish.

Dr. Christopher B. Howard, Class of 1991

"Dadgummit!"

Out of high school I was recruited to go to the Academy by the assistant coach Chan Gailey and the head coach Ken Hatfield. I really felt these were two of the finest men I had ever met, let alone football coaches. Little did I know that my future position coach and head coach, Fisher DeBerry, would be one of the most influential people that I have ever met.

As a player I used to get a kick out of Coach DeBerry's unique "Fisherisms." When he would get upset at us, he would never cuss but he would often yell "Garden Seed!" and "Dadgummit!" Or if you really messed up he would say, "My 92-year-old grandmama is better than that." When he was certain of something, he would tell us it would happen 99 times out of 10.

The best was when we went to Notre Dame in 1984, Coach DeBerry's first year as a head coach at Air Force. During Coach DeBerry's pre-game speech he told us, "There is no doubt in my mind that we can't beat these guys" and that "They had brought the green jerseys out for us."

Now I'm not sure if Coach really meant to tell us that he believed we couldn't beat them and even though they didn't wear their green jerseys, he still led us to a 21-7 victory in South Bend!

He is the most enthusiastic coach and person I have ever met. He utilized every second of time he had with his players. There were many afternoons when our pre-practice meeting consisted of the quarterbacks chasing Coach DeBerry down the hill to the practice fields. He would always be about 10 yards in front of us sprinting with a big grease board under his arm. We would have our pre-practice meeting on the field while the other positions sat in the air-conditioned field house sitting in nice comfortable chairs. However, I would learn to understand that his intense enthusiasm and passion for the game of football and the young men he would coach is what has made him the tremendous success that he is today. Practice was NEVER easy when Coach DeBerry was your position coach; the 25 minutes that he had just the quarterbacks was probably tougher than the Academy's basic training.

He even put the quarterbacks in harnesses and made us pull each other around the field until he would blow his whistle. At the time, I wasn't sure how that made us better quarterbacks, but it did make us tougher. He would make every drill as tough (often we felt unrealistic) as it could be. Then it would seem easy when we had to accomplish it during the game. I'll never forget the Friday nights before our games.

When most of the players were relaxing in their rooms watching "Dallas" or "SportsCenter," the quarterbacks would be up with Coach DeBerry in his hotel room. We would go over every possible scenario for what seemed like hours. He would have his manila folder that he still carries on game day that was full cover to cover with his scribbling of notes and plays. He always had us prepared for everything. It wouldn't surprise me if Marty Louthan's 45-yard spontaneous quarterback sneak in 1982 against Notre Dame wasn't a result of a Friday night meeting.

I really believe that I learned the most from Coach DeBerry when given the opportunity to coach on his staff. The first thing I realized is his relentless giving of his time for others. In staff meetings, Coach sometimes would say, " I couldn't sleep last night so I got up and did some correspondence." Even if some "Doodly Wompass" wrote and said, "Great win on Saturday," Coach always made time to get back with him—and anyone who takes time to write Coach.

After graduation I used to drop Coach DeBerry a note about once a year and was shocked when I would get a handwritten, personal note back from him every time. I used to think, "Wow, Coach DeBerry really must like me if he writes me back so much." It wasn't until later I realized how special a person he is to answer every piece of correspondence he receives.

The second thing I learned coaching under him is his ability to communicate and influence everyone he meets. From the little brother of a potential recruit to the four-star general, no one forgets Coach DeBerry after talking with him. He has been an inspiration and role model for me as I try to make a positive influence on young student athletes the way he impacted me.

Brian Knorr, Class of 1986, currently defensive coordinator, Ohio University

11

The Hardest Good-bye

My mother became ill after she retired. She was 62 years old. She had built a solid foundation for her future. Even though she didn't have much money, she used what she did have wisely. She bought some real estate and was earning revenue from that investment. She also had money put away because she never lived an extravagant lifestyle. So she was set.

Not having a lot to do once she retired gave her a lot of time to think about a lot of things.

She struggled for the next few years and went through some depression. She didn't understand nutrition and didn't eat right. She spent the last three years of her life in a wonderful nursing home. But she wasn't completely happy with that arrangement. That's a difficult thing because everyone has a vision of what retirement life is like.

But it was very difficult not to see her enjoy the fruits of her labor.

I felt badly for her because she had done so much for me. She was so committed and devoted to her mother, which was a great lesson for me in terms of being committed to her family. From her final years, I learned another lesson from her: to stop and smell the roses as often as possible through life.

My mother had worked her skin to the bone for four

decades. She never re-married though she had the chance. She wasn't really extroverted or outgoing, but she was always so physically attractive. And she was a beautiful person. She had so many opportunities to travel and do other things for herself. But over the years, she had given them up because she was either taking care of me or her mother. It broke my heart that I couldn't make it right because she had always made it right for me.

She had made so many sacrifices and given so much of herself for me. When she was in a nursing home, I felt bad that I couldn't press a button to put her in good health and let her enjoy everything.

She had always wanted to go to DisneyWorld because she was so young at heart. She would have really enjoyed that. But I was never able to do that for her because of how her health was deteriorating and that hurt me, not being able to help her realize some of her dreams because she made so many of my dreams possible.

She died on February 7, 1998, at age 77, of heart incapacitation—her heart just gave out. I guess you could say she died of a broken heart. It was really a combination of things that led to her passing, including the depression and the onset of Alzheimer's disease.

Just under six months before, on August 26, 1997 my grandmother died, just two days before her 100th birthday. So it didn't surprise me that my mother would pass early the next year because those two beautiful women had been so close, and I know that God wanted my mother to share in His Kingdom and joy with my grandmother.

My mother was proud of who she was, her parents and me. She had a limited world in tiny Cheraw. All she did was go to work and then read or watch TV at home at night, getting ready for the next day's work. Even on the weekends, her only big outing was going to church. Her whole world was contained basically within a 10-block area. But that was her world and she made the best of it, especially for her mother.

When my father died and our grandparents took us in, my mother obviously decided that she would take care of my grandparents when the time came. She was so committed to them because she had seen how committed they were to us. Since my mother had been so committed to me, I wanted to see her be the one on the other end of the commitment. So to see her suffer and not be happy was painful. She had to depend on other people for her existence in the end and that was very hard on her.

She was unable to reach the personal fulfillment that I had hoped for. With the expanded horizons I had through coaching and education—which she made possible for me—I wanted to make her feel the way she had made me feel. I wanted to give back to her some of what she had given to me.

She did get out to Colorado Springs a few times. I was able to take her to Cripple Creek, and we had some good memories around that time. But to her, a big event was a family picnic. It was always about family to her and she just loved being around Michelle and Joe, her grandchildren. It hurt her when she was too ill to make it out to Colorado for Joe's high school graduation in 1988. She had made it to Michelle's graduation, but she just wasn't well enough to make Joe's. That hurt her more than anything. She wasn't able to do the simple things late in her life, and as her body failed her and she had to have her every need taken care of, it was very hard on her.

I had seen my grandmother live to age 99, and even in the final few years her mind was so sharp. My grandmother and I had a good conversation on the phone one day when she was 95. She expected the end was near, but her faith never waned.

"I know where I'm going and I can't wait to get there," she told me. "I want to be with the Good Lord and my husband."

My grandmother and I had a good talk that day. She told me, "It didn't matter what we had accumulated here on earth. All that we take to heaven is what we've done for others on earth."

That made a profound impression on me. And it is so very true. It doesn't matter what you have in your bank account or if you have four cars in your four-car garage. What mattered, my grandmother pointed out that day, is that while we didn't have a big house or any big possessions, our family was well thought of and we had a good name. I never got to have that talk with my mother, though I know she is in Heaven with God and her pain is finally gone.

12

Our Heisman Trophy

The Heisman Trophy of Air Force Football is the Brian Bullard Memorial Award—an Air Force player can win no higher honor.

This award is given annually at the Football Award's banquet and presented by Brian's mother, Betty Bullard.

Let me tell you who Brian Bullard was and how he lives on in our program. Brian graduated from Air Academy High School, located on the U.S. Air Force Academy in Colorado Springs. He came to the Academy the following year. He's another one of those kids that could have played and done pretty well for one of the state's smaller schools. But he didn't get a lot of attention from the bigger Division I-A schools. We welcomed him aboard because we already knew the kind of character he had.

He played on the junior varsity as a freshman. In the off-season, he was fierce in the weight room, building his muscles and raising the level of his conditioning. He made the varsity and lettered in 1983. The city of Colorado Springs was very proud that one of its own was a key member of our defense and perhaps even a standout eventually.

During Thanksgiving vacation in November of 1983, Brian and his girlfriend, Cadet Dianne Williams of Cameron, Missouri, were returning home to the Academy, driving through Kansas. Four miles east of Goodland, Kansas, Brian and Dianne were stuck in a blinding snowstorm. Driving on a closed interstate, no one passed by until the next morning. Dead in the car were Brian and Dianne, of carbon monoxide poisoning. The loss hit the Academy hard. Dianne was on the golf team and very well-liked. Brian, of course, was a favorite on the football team.

Brian was an inspiration because he was the epitome of teamwork and commitment—as well as being dedicated to the team. He didn't have a ton of natural skill or physical skill, but he worked hard. Brian had a positive impact on our team. I asked Brian's parents for permission to establish a memorial award to honor and challenge our future players.

His award is the pinnacle in our program. The standards for the award are very high: unselfishness, 110-percent effort, total team commitment and being proud of your role on the team, whether you're a starter or not.

We have a board outside our football offices that our players pass by every day as they head out to practice, with two big pictures of Brian—one in his Air Force uniform and the other in his football uniform. Between those two portraits are pictures of the players who have won the award since it was established after the 1984 season. The players on that board weren't highly recruited by big schools. They weren't the biggest or fastest or quickest or strongest when they got here. They made up for it in desire and heart. I could take those 17 players, whose pictures are on that board, and whip anyone in the country. I don't care who the college is or where they are ranked. The sacrifice and commitment of these kids is beyond what anyone could ever expect. They all, like Brian, had incredible character.

The day Brian died was so devastating. I can't think of anything harder to deal with than losing a child. Lu Ann and

I have talked about it, but we can't grasp what someone goes through when a child passes. But I have been so impressed with how Betty Bullard has continued in her faith. This only strengthened her commitment to God. She's just a beautiful Christian woman.

"Good things happen to good people"

When my son, Brian Bullard, was being recruited by the Air Force Academy, he often talked about an assistant offensive coach who had a funny accent. Of course, he was talking about Fisher DeBerry. Brian had traveled a good bit in his 18 years but not in the southern part of the United States. Thus he was not acquainted with anything resembling Fisher's now very famous accent.

But Fisher already had made an impression on Brian.

Brian thought Fisher was "one neat guy" who was going to do wonders with the Air Force offense. When Brian was recruited, Ken Hatfield was the head coach and Fisher was the offensive coordinator. Brian was recruited as a nose guard/defensive tackle.

I had met Fisher at several football events at the Academy between when Brian started his first year at the Academy and Brian's death in November of 1983. But I didn't really get to know Fisher until after Brian's death. Ken Hatfield and an assistant coach told me of Brian's death the night it happened. A day or two later, Fisher and Ken came by our house to pay their respects and offer any needed help. My mother and Brian's other grandparents, as well as an aunt and uncle, were here by then. As I remember, we all had a very nice visit. Of course, we discussed football some and the upcoming bowl season. The next opportunity I had to visit with Fisher was in the spring of 1984. By this time Ken had gone to the University of Arkansas as head coach and Fisher was the very popular new Head Coach of the Air Force Academy.

In April of 1984, Brian's father and I met with Fisher and the late Colonel John Clune, then the Academy's outstanding athletic director, to discuss the development of the "Brian Bullard Award." While I do not remember the conversation in great detail, I do remember how important it was to Fisher and Colonel Clune that it become a very significant award in the Air Force athletic department and for the football team. We had several conversations and finally the format of the award was developed—the criteria for the award, when it would be awarded and so on.

The first award was made in the winter of 1985 at the annual Denver/Colorado Springs Quarterback Club football banquet, at which time honors were distributed based on the season from the previous fall. Steve Kelly was the first recipient of the Brian Bullard Award. Steve and Brian were very good friends and everyone was extremely pleased. So we were underway developing the tradition of the Brian Bullard award.

The announcement of the winner is always at the very end of the banquet. Fisher reads the criteria for the winner, and reminds the audience of the past winners. I try to say something about the award and the past winners before I announce that year's winner. The winner always gets a standing ovation. Fisher used to tell me quite some time in advance who won the award. I loved being a part of the secret. But as the significance of the award developed and it was discussed more and more in Falcon football circles, I started to worry that by knowing so far in advance who won that I would accidentally spill the beans, or make the mistake of telling someone who would leak word of the winner!

So for a few years Fisher would tell me the evening of the football banquet, telling me a bit about the player selected. That worked great for a year or two. However, I found myself spending the rest of the evening trying to figure out what I wanted to say about the award and the recipient instead of enjoying the program and highlight film!

Now we have a routine where I stop by Fisher's office about 10 days before the banquet. He tells me about the winner, and then we chat and visit—and talk some football. Then I can plan my remarks in advance and still enjoy the program.

Fisher will tell you that he can "take that group of players who won the Brian Bullard Award and whip anyone in the country. I don't care who it is!"

To say Fisher DeBerry has a lot to do with the development of the Brian Bullard Award is an understatement. But then, Fisher is the reason Air Force Academy football is the success story that it is. It makes me extremely proud to tell people that my son played in the Air Force program, met the standards of youngsters in the program, and no doubt would have been a very successful officer in the Air Force.

Time does march on. Brian's niece and nephew now attend the banquet with me every year. They always want to go say hello to Fisher. And Fisher remembers them, inquires about how they're doing in school and so on. And they love telling their friends about those conversations.

Fisher is such a positive influence to everyone who meets him or knows him. He is a walking example of good things happening to good people.

It is no secret that losing a child is one of the worst things that can happen to any parent. And we all pray our youngster will not be forgotten. I am so very fortunate that, thanks to Fisher DeBerry, my son will be remembered in the most positive of ways.

Betty Bullard, Colorado Springs, Colorado

13

Those Around You

As I was putting together this book, I ran into a man named Dick Fanning, who coached my son, Joe, at Air Academy High School here in Colorado Springs. Coach Fanning had a profound influence on my son and gave a lot of time to Joe's development both as a baseball player and a person. Coach Fanning spent countless hours helping Joe learn about baseball and life. I'm grateful for that, as is Joe's mother.

That made me reflect on some of the many who have influenced my life so much. These influences really shaped who I am as a Christian, father, husband, coach and teacher.

Jack Summers was an outstanding player at Furman University. Jack was the first to teach me about the importance of being a family man. He was not just a good coach. He knew the fundamentals of the game, but he was also one tough guy. He was in my church and that lesson always stuck with me— the importance of having your family in your church.

Ed Bost helped spur my interest in coaching. Actually, he dated my aunt for a while. He played at Appalachian State where I would end up as an assistant coach down the road a ways.

Bob Bell coached me in three sports in high school. He wasn't married at the time. But he was an immaculate dresser and a real professional. I didn't have my dad around, and coach Bell took a lot of personal interest in me. That was important, especially at that point in my life, to have such a positive male role model whom I could talk to and learn from. He really got me excited about coaching. I learned a lot from him about organizational skills and how to treat people.

My coaches in college had a huge influence on me, none more than Jim Brakefield, who was my baseball coach at Wofford. He also was the defensive coordinator. He had a tremendous competitiveness and work ethic, yet he was hard-nosed and tough. However, his players loved him because he was always fair. Jim was like a Daddy to me. I learned so much from him.

The basketball coach at Wofford—who was also an assistant football coach—was Gene Alexander. He's in the Hall of Fame in South Carolina. When I went back to coach at Wofford, Gene and I ran the defense together. The rapport he had with his players was something special. I observed the way he interacted and managed his players.

Jim Wall is someone I coached with at the high school level. I knew of him years earlier because we used to scrimmage his high school team when he was at McClenaghan and I was at Cheraw. He was one of the most respected coaches in the state. I thought he was one of the sharpest people I ever met. We coached together when I got out of the Army and had a lot of success.

Colonel John Clune was an amazing man. He was the athletic director at the Air Force Academy when Ken Hatfield hired me. Colonel Clune had a perception of seeing the big picture and seeing things down the road. He took the Academy to a level of athletic success that could never have been imagined before he took over as athletic director. He always was listening and learning and then applying those things at the Academy.

He reminded me many times to not get so engrossed in your work that you forget your family. He really took time for his kids and his wonderful wife, Pat, which was a great inspiration for me. He knew the commitment that had to be made across the board—equipment, facilities, conferences, and even coaches and recruiting. But what made him the most special was his caring and humor. He died of cancer shortly after retiring from the Air Force and his brilliant, long career. He often shared with me his plans for retirement, and it saddened me to think that he was never able to do any of the things he had spent hours describing to me. But he is in heaven now, and I'm sure he's smiling upon us to this day.

Of course, Ken Hatfield has been a good friend and a big part of my entire modus operandi. I always admired his values and faith. Obviously, I would never have come to the Air Force Academy had it not been for him. He was one of the reasons I became head coach—not just because he left and recommended me, but because I knew the foundation of the program here was solid because of his values and beliefs. It was Ken who taught me the absolute necessity and importance of surrounding yourself with good people.

The late Jim Conboy, our head trainer for many years, meant a lot to me. What a great role model he was for me, and what a great friendship we enjoyed. When he passed away a few years ago, it was a great personal loss. We honored him by wearing a decal on our helmets that said "Doc." He was very much a part of the success of that team the year after he died as he was on every team. His wife had died during their children's formative years, and he worked hard at everything he did. He had such a commitment to his kids.

He also had a commitment to the players here. There was no such thing as a clock to Jim—he worked to the bone. He stayed as long as the players needed him and came in as early as needed, all the while raising his wonderful children.

On a different note, these men were the reason I stayed involved in sports. My mother never saw me play much in high school or college. And my grandmother and mother didn't know a lot about sports. Heck, neither did Granddaddy. So these coaches were the ones who really fed my interest and motivated me to continue. Their encouragement was priceless. So were their contributions to my upbringing on how to be a proper young man.

I've had friends like Bob McLean, a close Christian brother, whom I coached with in high school, and fellow coaches and Christians like Cal McCombs, Chan Gailey and Jimmy Grobe, who have added so much to my life. I want to mention all the men I coached with or had fellowship with at this point, but there simply aren't enough pages in this book to list them all. But I want all of you to know that I thank the Good Lord often for your friendship and fellowship and great work.

My minister has been a big mentor to me—and not just because Ed Beck is 6-feet, 8-inches tall! Ed was an All-American center at the University of Kentucky when they won the national championship under Coach Adolph Rupp.

You have experiences in high school and college as a player and coach that you learn from. We don't come up with much that is original. We gather bits and pieces here and there. I've done that through coaching and teaching. I've had some great teachers and coaches in the classroom, on the athletic field and spiritually.

All of the people in my life—many of whom are not listed by name—have contributed to who I am as a person and to my style and manner of doing things. I have learned from them and emulated their role model.

I believe God puts everyone in your life for a reason. Sometimes it is to learn how to do things—and on other occasions it is to learn how not to do things. These people have provided shining examples to me. All of my friends, mentors and the like have amazed me with the consistency of their Christian walk. They are not tossed and turned by the whims of people.

They've also helped show me the keys to be happy and successful in life.

"99 times out of 10"

As I think back on my experience with Coach Fisher DeBerry at the Air Force Academy, there are two main characteristics that stand out about him. First, he is a great motivator. Second, he is a great family man.

In 1992, I was an assistant coach at Baylor University with Ken Rucker.

I asked Ken, "What's the best place you've ever coached?

"Without a doubt, the Air Force Academy," Rucker answered.

Four years later, there was an opening on the Academy staff. I was fortunate that Ken thought enough of me to call Coach DeBerry to recommend me for the job.

During the off-season conditioning program, I was able to see what kind of motivator Coach DeBerry is. This segment of the off-season training is held in "the cage," at the indoor Cadet Field House at the Academy. It is called "the cage" because of the nets that hang down from the ceiling.

Each coach is assigned a station. The players are divided into groups and they rotate through each station. After learning the routine and setup, we went down to the indoor field. As the players started lining up to stretch, about 30 women— much to my amazement—were also lined up. I wondered what was going on. The other coaches didn't seem concerned. I asked Coach DeBerry, and he told me that the program we ran at that time of year was open to any Academy cadet. "Coach them like you would anyone else," Coach DeBerry told me.

Those women went through every drill like any other player. The message from Coach DeBerry was clear: No one is different, or better, or worse, than anyone else. We are all the same. We get treated the same regardless of nationality or race, gender or anything else.

At the end of one of the cage sessions, I was able to hear one of Coach's well-known "Fisher-isms." We were all in a group and he was telling the team, "You know, 99 times out of 10, the best-conditioned team wins." I was thinking, "Those numbers aren't right." But no one else even blinked—they had heard Coach say it a million times and knew what he meant, so they just nodded in agreement.

Along with conditioning, Coach DeBerry believes in the power of positive thinking. Every player—and every person—associated with that program believes that they will win when they step on the field. I remember playing several well-known, high-profile teams my first year at the Academy, such as the University of Washington and Colorado State University. I'd be walking around during warm-ups before the game, thinking, "We don't have any players who look as good as our opponent's players." But I also knew every player we had believed we would win. I'd look in our players' eyes before the game and what I saw was so reassuring. Their confidence gave me a sense of well-being. I could see our guys had no doubt in their minds that we were going to win. And we did, winning 12 of 13 games that year.

Coach DeBerry is constantly selling the concept of "The Falcon Family." You can see that bond throughout the program—it's a very unique bond. All the players call each other their "brother." It's not uncommon to hear these young men say they "love their brother."

They know the worst thing they can do is let their brother down and they talk about that before games.

Off the field, Coach DeBerry makes everyone's family feel special. He involves the coaches' families in many occasions, especially holidays. My wife and kids have received either cards or calls from Coach on their birthdays. On Thursdays when I was coaching at the Academy, my wife would bring our children, Dillon (then 6) and Sydney (4) to practice. After practice ended, Coach DeBerry would play football with the kids. It was amazing to see this 60-year-old coaching legend roll in the grass with a bunch of smiling and laughing children. Because of those interactions, my son's goal and dream is to grow up and be a Fighting Falcon.

I am sure one of the reasons Coach DeBerry has had so much continuity on his coaching staff is because of this kind of attention given to the value and importance of family. It's probably a big part of the program's success as well.

He cares about others as though they are his family, too. Indeed, I remember every week at least once in our morning meeting, Coach DeBerry would have a card for us to sign for someone somewhere in the country who had some hardship. We'd all sign the card, hoping it would bring some good feelings to whomever was suffering adversity.

The two years at the Academy were very special to my family. I accumulated a great amount of knowledge. I learned not only about the "Fishbone" offense, but also about spiritual and social lessons dealing with life.

There is no doubt in my mind that the Air Force Academy will be successful for years to come because of the values and principles Coach DeBerry has instilled in the program.

Before I went there, I had heard coach upon coach say how "special" it is to coach at the Air Force Academy with Coach DeBerry. But until you experience it, you can't fully comprehend the truth and breadth of that statement. It was really hard to leave. Had I been 10 years older and further along in my career with different goals, I probably would've stayed indefinitely. I certainly would never rule out returning.

Larry Fedora, Offensive Coordinator, Middle Tennessee State University

14

Character

Character is a summation of who you are as a person. Character is how you act and who you are when no one else is looking. Certainly, most of your character comes from your upbringing and the decisions you make, especially at the forks you face along life's road.

I don't believe anyone is simply born with good character. Your environment and the people after whom you model yourself, are what determines your character. The accountability and standards you are raised around—and what comes from within—determine your character.

Once you are through the initial formative years, you make choices in your life that come from the character in your heart and soul.

Good character does so much for a person. If you are of sound, high character, the tough choices don't seem so tough and even the trickiest of forks in the road provide an obvious choice most of the time.

You make sacrifices because of your character. My mother and grandparents instilled that in me. You are a product of all of your experiences. You can't tell someone in words about your character. However, your words and actions tell all anyone needs to know about you and your character.

And there's no better forum for character than adversity.

How you deal with the hand life dealt you goes a long way in determining your character.

I could have used not having a dad or something else as an excuse. Maybe, if I'd have had a drinking problem, I could have said, "Well, I just never got over the fact that my father had a drinking problem and so I've got it—not my fault," but that's not the truth. The fact of the matter is we all have baggage that we have to deal with and that's the key: Deal with it, whether it means discussing it in counseling with a therapist or with the minister from your church. You can overcome your past. You MUST overcome the past. By the same token, you can build on the things that were good in your life and the good things that you picked up from those who raised you. I credit my work ethic to my mother, my responsibility to my grandmother and grandfather, my spirituality to my grandmother and my sense of financial accountability to my grandfather.

Life is never easy or so the age-old adage goes. But the truth of the matter is, life is no harder—or easier—than we make it most of the time. By surrounding yourself with good people and having positive role models in your life, you can see the right way to do things. You learn things that make your life not just easier, but improve the overall quality of your life.

That's why life is not always about WHAT you know, but WHO you know. Not just because you have a great network that can help you with your career—which helps and I've been blessed by it—but the key in WHO you know is WHAT you learn and how you can apply it. So if you know the right kind of people and experience mentorship or fellowship with them, you will remain one step ahead in the game of life.

BUILDING BRIDGES

You build a bridge step by step, plank by plank. That is because life is a journey, not a singular great leap to a destination. You have to have some foundation or some plan or engineering design to build on the experiences you have from your early childhood, church, school and even sports. That's why it's so critical to give young people today good experiences as children.

They are building their own bridges. They won't reach the end of that bridge until the last day of their lives, and hopefully that will springboard them to an eternal life. But it all starts with the foundation. The foundation in my life is my faith and the assurances the "master playbook"—the Bible—gives us.

If you don't build the bridge one step at a time, you are creating a dangerous base for your future, likewise if you put in a soft or inferior board. If the board is not firm and sound, then you run the chance of hitting that board again and you can fall, perhaps hard. If that inferior plank goes out and you miss that step, it can ruin the entire bridge. You fall into one of life's rivers or valleys. And if you don't drown, you at least become very wet and uncomfortable.

If your bridge is not sound, you should remember that we have a strong and understanding Father watching over us. We can go to Him for guidance and then repair the bridge—making it better and stronger—and then continue our journey.

Before you even start building your bridges, make sure your foundations are set in good faith, values and good beliefs. Because if you build in sand, you might get washed away. If the foundation is rock solid, it will survive the elements and the test of time. And you will survive even the harshest of storms.

KEEPING THE FAITH

The greatest test of a person's faith is when they find themselves on a fence. Does a person jump to the other side of the fence when there's a chance for social and popular approval? Or does he stand by his beliefs knowing he might have to endure criticism and grief? It's easy to have morals and principles when it's "cool" or "popular" or it is the current trend. It's harder when there's pressure, but that's a test of your faith, and you'll find out how true and deep your faith runs on those occasions. In my mind, there's no room for fence-riders.

TEAMWORK

Teamwork is commitment. It means everyone is committed to the same thing. You can't be successful without it. The epitome of teamwork is when you have a group of people who don't care about getting the credit.

Teamwork is a group of people who really care for each other. They are there for each other through the good times and bad, which in football might be the wins and losses. The thing we as a coaching staff try to drive home is that we're all brothers and that we do care about each other.

It truly hurts you when your brother is hurting. It's always been good to see our players rally around each other when someone has adversity on the field, off the field, in the classroom or in life. We pray for each other when someone gets hurt or has an ailing family member.

Corporate America puts together its structure and organization from the framework and foundation just like the military does. The military is so organized. Everyone has a responsibility and a job to do. And everyone else along the line is depending on everyone else to do his or her jobs. One weak link weakens the chain. Two weak links render the chain useless. The link after you is counting on you to get the job done right, and the link before you is counting on you to get the job done right and on time so as not to slow it down either.

Football is the same thing. You miss an assignment and the guy who took on two blocks next to you did it for nothing. The guy next to you who was executing his responsibility has to give that up to cover for the job you left undone. A breakdown doesn't end with the person who commits it initially. It works its way back up and down the line. It demoralizes those who hold up their end of the deal. With the right sense of responsibility and accountability, it's not hard to come through for your team, no matter what job you do or what sport you play. Just remember, if it's a team environment, then it's not about just you no matter the circumstances. All of the credit and blame are shared equally.

If you don't have a good team concept, you won't be too successful. There must be just one heartbeat, all working and striving toward the same goals.

DEDICATION AND DISCIPLINE

Dedication, discipline and commitment go hand in hand. Dedication means being willing to do whatever it takes to see the job completed. That's all we ever ask out of our players, that they play to the last play of the game as hard as they know how. That's why we say that we've never lost a game at the Air Force Academy. Time might have run out on us, but we've never lost. That's our attitude.

Time might run out, but we believe we can win every game. Dedication means playing as hard as you can on the last play of the game as you did on the first play of the game. When you commit yourself to doing a job, you don't just accept the more pleasing aspects of it. There's probably 68 percent of my job that is far less pleasing than the 32 percent I really enjoy. But it's more than well worth it to work as hard as I can through the aspects that are not my favorite.

Discipline also means being giving of your time. And I do want to give of my time. I receive a lot of correspondence from people of all walks of life. I know that they thought enough of me that they were willing to give of their time to write me. So I want, and need, to write them back. A lot of times that will mean getting up earlier in the morning for me, but that's part of being disciplined.

OPTIMISM

If you aren't optimistic, the sky is not as bright. The days seem longer. The simple pleasures are overlooked. Folks focus on what they don't have instead of what they do have. Optimism is a key to achievement, and it says a lot about your character as well.

I went to visit my hometown of Cheraw a few years back. I went to a little league baseball game because I had a little cousin playing.

In typical fashion, there were little kids standing on the field, looking at the sky and some with their hands in their pockets.

We arrived a little bit late and had to park outside of centerfield. So I asked the centerfielder, "What's the score?"

"It's 13-0," he said.

"Boy," I replied, "things don't look too good."

"Shucks, Mister," the little guy said, "we ain't even been to bat yet."

He was optimistic that his team could meet and exceed what the other team had done. He viewed the challenge as an opportunity for his team to practice the fundamentals they had learned to get back in the ball game. He didn't see it as an obligation to go through the motions and see the game called early because of the mercy rule.

There's a story about a mom and dad who had two little boys, Optimist and Pessimist.

The mother and father wanted to change Pessimist's attitude. So one year for Christmas, they bought him everything he asked for and more—just everything you could possibly imagine. The boy bounced from toy to toy.

"This new ball is too small."

"This little car is the wrong color."

"This baseball bat is too light."

"This glove doesn't fit."

"This coat itches."

The parents had gotten Optimist just a little bag and put some small trinkets in it. The father realized they had left that present out on the porch, and he rushed out to get it. He gave it to the boy, but as it turned out, the father brought in the wrong bag. The bag he brought in had a bunch of horse manure that he had scrapped off of his boots the night before.

Little Optimist opened the bag and saw the horse manure.

"All right!" the boy yelled. "Where's the pony?"

He thought he was getting a pony because he always made the best of everything. That's my attitude; you find the best in any situation. It's fun to be an optimist.

REALIZING POTENTIAL

Potential isn't worth a hill of beans if it is not actualized.

We talk about the potential to be a good team, but potential is one thing. Actualization is something completely different. If potential is the letter "A" in the alphabet, then actualization is "Z." They are that far apart, at least in raw form.

In between A and Z is a lot of hard work and sacrifice, the

necessities to realize potential. I've seen schools with top 10 recruiting classes finish with back-to-back losing records. These kids and coaches didn't understand they were part of a team. The teams that are good in the little things and intangibles are going to be successful—not the most talented.

We had teams that returned a large number of lettermen, teams that conditioned and lifted weights really hard, and we've thought, "Wow, we're going to win the Commander-in-Chief's Trophy and the conference title." Then we ended up with six or seven wins. Why? We didn't realize our potential. We didn't have the round pegs in the round holes or the square pegs in the square holes. Somewhere along the line, several people in the program were not doing their jobs.

There have been other years where we thought we'd go .500 and we ended up winning eight or nine games and going to a bowl. Why? Because these kids had more character than we ever thought. They took every challenge as a mission and executed their assignments with a love for their brothers.

That's why character is so important. Character is the essence of life and of being successful. Kids we've honored since 1985, the competitive kinds of people—had a load of character—they were not necessarily the most talented kids.

I think humility is very important. I never was a great enough athlete to be conceited, but I wouldn't have been conceited had I been a great athlete. I'm thankful for what I have, and I realize it is all through God's grace and goodness. Humility is our gift to God. What it means to me is this: What can I do for others? Others are a lot more important to me, than I am to myself.

In coaching, I don't mind doing a lot of the work, but I'm never going to put myself out there in front getting the credit.

You do have to be confident, and you want your team to have an aura of confidence around it. But there is a fine line between being prepared and being overconfident. There's a fine line between being self-assured and being arrogant. And arrogance is something I detest.

At the same time, there's a beauty in someone who is secure in who they are, what they can accomplish, how they prepared and practiced, and what they are seeking to achieve.

Once you achieve a goal, you feel a sense of pride. That's when the ultimate satisfaction of your efforts come. I can stand back and look at some of the things we've been able to accomplish at the Academy, and I'm sure when I'm retired I'll be proud. At this point, I haven't reflected on the numbers or occasions. Right now, I'm just looking at expanding goals and horizons, seeing where we've been, how we got to where we are, and what's the best course for our next destinations.

Pride can be a negative thing if used and applied the wrong way. Misdirected pride can ruin friendships, relationships, teams and companies. Too much pride directed the wrong way can make you think you're better than you really are. And from the lofty perches born from these illusions come horrible falls. Pride directed the right way can be contagious. If you get a group of players who have a lot of pride in each other and what they are doing, then you are probably not just going to meet your goals, but exceed them as well. There's nothing more exciting than seeing your highest goal within your grasp. It's not just a testament to how far you've come. It says a lot about who you are, the sacrifices you've made and the hard work you've displayed.

LEADERSHIP

As I wrote earlier, the Academy exists to produce leaders for the Air Force, who in turn protect our country and our freedoms.

That's why what we're doing is so meaningful every

single day. A leader can help someone do something that they don't think they can do.

A good leader can instill and develop confidence in those around him or her.

Leadership is also getting out front and pulling, as contrasted with getting behind and pushing. If you have a rope and you push it, the rope buckles. However, if you get in front and pull, the rope is going to stay in a straight line. How do you want to get where you are going? In a straight line. That's the shortest distance, which is important in ventures where time is a concern or there is competition involved.

Leaders are willing to step out front and not worry about criticism or people questioning and abusing them. Every season I get abused for being a stupid coach, but it never keeps me from wanting to get back in there the next day. To be a good leader, you shouldn't have to talk about it a lot—people see it in you. Hopefully, the way you do things—the way you live your life and interact with people—will make others want to follow you. When they want to follow you, then you've found the definition of leadership.

COMMITMENT

Commitment is part of who you are. If you give someone your word, you have to realize what that means. Your word is the most prized possession you have. If I tell someone I will do something or be somewhere, I will do everything within my power to do it. Commitment is finishing what you begin. After we had our first losing season, I had to ask for a deep commitment out of our football team. As it turned out, I ended up receiving an offer to take another job a few months later. I didn't take that job because I had asked for such a big commitment out of our players. What kind of person would I have been had I asked for that and then bolted on those kids?

LOYALTY

To me, telling someone they are loyal is the greatest compliment you can give.

I illustrate that with a little tale that Bill Yung tells about when Grant Teaff was the head coach at Baylor and Bill was an assistant.

They had a bad season at Baylor that year. Grant was working himself to the bone, staying in the office until all hours of the night. Bill felt Grant had to get out. Bill invited Grant to go hunting several times. Grant said he just didn't have the time and kept putting Bill off for the hunting. But Bill kept on talking. Finally, Bill said, "I won't accept no for an answer."

Grant said all right, and he made arrangements with a booster to hunt on the booster's land. Bill went by to pick up Grant, and they drove 50 miles down the interstate and 40 miles through the backroads of farmland. Grant told Bill to stay in the car so Grant could go up to the house to thank the booster for letting them hunt there. The booster consoled Grant, "You guys are doing a good job. You're doing things the right way. Don't worry about how this football season went. We're proud to have you guys as coaches and glad to have you here. You are going to win big very soon"

"I appreciate your encouragement. Thanks for having us," Grant says.

"Before you go, can you do me a favor, coach?" the man asked.

"Sure, what?" Grant questioned.

"That sickly 25-year-old mule over there by the barn has been in the family forever," the man says. "He needs to be put out of his misery, but I can't shoot him. He's diseased and won't get any better. Would you do it?"

"No problem," Grant replied.

The booster headed back in the house, and Grant was still thinking he had to get back to the office. So, he decided to act like the conversation with the booster didn't go that well so they could hit the road. Grant went back to the truck.

"Bill, let's get out of here," Grant said. "That man doesn't want us hunting here. He thinks our program is so bad and that we're terrible coaches. See that mule over there, I think I'll shoot him. I'm gonna shoot that old codger's mule."

Grant grabs his weapon and shoots the mule and then gets back in the truck. He looked and Bill was not in the truck anymore. Grant heard two gunshots and then saw Bill running toward the truck with his rifle.

"Let's get out of here, coach!" Bill said. "I just shot two of his cows!"

What that tells me is: That's total loyalty.

BALANCE

You have to have balance in your life—a sense of being well-rounded.

If you just focus on one area, you can get so overwhelmed and so engrossed that you don't see or appreciate other things. That often leads—particularly when things don't go your way—to a lot of frustration and disappointment. However, if you have balance and can enjoy other things, you will be happier.

The spill-off from the happiness from one venture, spills over into others, even into relationships. Likewise, if something isn't going well and you are burned out or have hit a wall, you have another avenue to direct your creativity and drive. You can achieve meaningful things in many areas of your life.

A singular interest or pursuit can destroy you even if you

master it. You will, at some point, become either burned out or lack other challenges. Neither is a good feeling.

That's why I've always looked to take more classes and have other hobbies.

PERSPECTIVE AND PRAYER

Another important factor in our program's success is that we have a chaplain as part of our program. I realized that need very quickly.

Back in 1984, we played San Diego State at Falcon Stadium in my first game as head coach. We won, 34-16, and I was just so emotionally spent afterward. I like to sit alone in the locker room after the game and reflect, but I have to deal with the media. I usually have a pretty good size group of people waiting to see me after the game. So I honored those commitments. Another commitment is that we go out as a staff after the game. All the coaches bring their wives and children. I don't want the wives to worry about cooking after a game, so we go somewhere fun where the kids can eat all the Jello they want and we can all relax.

I got home that night and felt exhausted. The phone rang and the news wasn't good. One of our players, Steve Rafferty—a very special young man—had played his heart out that day. The phone call was about his brother. His brother had been killed in a motorcycle accident that day. I had recruited Steve personally out of Arizona, so I knew his family.

I knew he needed some support. On the way to go see Steve, I stopped and picked up our chaplain. We had to find Steve, give him our support, love and prayers. We finally found Steve and spent a number of hours with him until he could fly home.

That made me realize the importance of having spiritual support as well as a spiritual mentor for our team.

From that day on, we've always had a team chaplain. That person travels with us and comes to our games and practices. Our players develop a great bond with this person, who is—in my estimation—a lot more important than the head football coach.

We developed a Share Time on our team. It used to be on Saturday morning, but we've since moved it to Friday night. Ken Hatfield started it when he was here.

We sit down together and give thanks for our gifts and opportunities. It's a time for us to keep the game in its proper perspective. The chaplain leads this. He and the Fellowship of Christian Athletes help get someone to speak to our team at this time. We have a lot of athletes or coaches who come in and share their thoughts with us. I think it's important for the players—and all of us—to learn from other people for our own growth. Share Time has been a great inspiration to us.

STEPS TO THE TOP

If you are going to be successful, you can never forget about the fundamentals—the little things. You have to be committed to the fundamentals. If you excel at the fundamentals and "little" things, you will win most of your games on the field and in life.

We want our players and staff to "expect to win." I believe you win with good people and positive attitudes. We'll work hard at it, but we also know that no one will ever exceed his own expectations. So, we set high goals because that is an expectation for which they will reach. We want the tradition and expectations in the program to be high.

You have to dream big. You have to have big visions and not limit yourself. A major corporation has a saying, "If you can dream it, we can make it." That's my way of thinking. If you dream it and can envision it—and if you are willing to put forth the effort—we can do anything. However, it takes everybody being committed. You have to continually expand your horizons, goal and expectations.

MAKING A DIFFERENCE

We don't have egos on our team or among our coaching staff. We all have a job to do. Whether it's a student manager, a video person, a third-team player, a coach, a starter or an administrative support person, we all have unique and important responsibilities. No one job is more important than the other.

Every single day our players and staff pass by a sign that reads, "You make the difference." That means no matter what your job is, it is your attitude toward your responsibility and your commitment to excellence that is going to contribute to this team. Everyone has a job to do and we expect everyone to take exceptional pride doing the jobs with quality and pride.

I really relate that to the military because the military itself is a large team. I've traveled to so many military bases throughout the world that I see how small the military family really is and that it is just a close-knit fraternity. I see how people care about their co-workers. I'll be at one base one day and another the next day and almost without fail, I will hear someone say, "Oh, you saw Captain so-and-so yesterday? I was stationed with him at a base 10 years ago."

It's also heart-warming to see players stationed alongside other players and Academy classmates at bases. I've had so many tell me how their football experiences have related positively to their military careers.

There's no better example of that than Scott Thomas. He was an All-American defensive back for us. During the Gulf War, he was shot down. He was within 75 yards of being picked up by the Iraqis. The media asked later how scared he was. Scott said, "I wasn't near as worried about the Iraqis as I was about Notre Dame's toss sweep when I was playing football at the Academy." Scott went on to talk about all the lessons he learned in football at the Academy, how his Survival, Evasion, Resistance and Escape Training after his freshman year helped him survive behind enemy lines, as did his experiences in the football program. The young man is a hero.

Ironically, who was among the group rescuing Scott? One of his former classmates at the Academy. The classmate was willing to give his life to save his "brother." That commitment and the commitment Scott Thomas showed in his courageous mission are beyond words. Like we say, "Brothers are hard to beat." If you shoot down Scott Thomas' plane, his brothers are coming to save him, and they'll be back the next day to even the score.

I harp on the "brothers are hard to beat" thing until I'm out of breath. That comes from my small town upbringing. We had a set of brothers in town and if you were going to fight one of the brothers and you beat him, you'd better be ready to fight his other brother, and the other one after that and so on. That's what brothers do.

Epilogue:
Point After, by Mike Burrows,
The Denver Post
Faith, Family and the Falcons

A few years ago, I coined that phrase to describe what's most important to Air Force Academy football coach Fisher DeBerry.

Friend—I am proud and flattered, that Fisher considers me one. Especially when many high-profile coaches consider the sports writers who cover their teams to be friends.

Having covered Fisher's AFA teams on a beat-writer basis from 1985-88 and again from 1996-97, and on a sidebar basis in other years through 1998, all while writing for the Colorado Springs Gazette, I had the opportunity to see a man from a fatherless home in tiny Cheraw, South Carolina, become as important to his school as the breathtaking Cadet Chapel, as important to his profession as the breath-operated whistle.

You watch Tony Gwynn hit a baseball and you realize he was put on this planet to hit a baseball. You see Mother Theresa care for the sick and the poor and you realize she was put on this planet to care for the sick and the poor. You watch John Elway throw a football and you realize he was put on this planet to throw a football. You read what Rick Reilly writes and you realize he was put on this planet to write.

Fisher DeBerry was put on this planet to coach football

and, by doing so, positively impact the lives of those around him.

I believed it the first year I saw him coach, in 1985, when the Falcons bolted to a 10-0 start, won a share of the Western Athletic Conference championship, beat Texas in the Bluebonnet Bowl, finished 12-1 and were ranked as high as No. 5 in the final national polls.

I still believe it. And not just because, after 16 seasons, he's the winningest coach in the history of service-academy football with a 126-69-1 (.645) record and victories over Notre Dame, Washington, Texas, Mississippi State and Ohio State.

I believe it because his players love playing for him. Always have.

"Coach DeBerry didn't just make me a better player. He made me a better person," Pat Evans, one of the best fullbacks in AFA history, once told me.

I believe it because Fisher introduced me to the goofy word "slobberknocker" As in: "That was a slobberknocker of a game."

I believe it because Fisher introduced me to the goofy phrase "changing gears in the middle of the stream." As in: "We can't be changing gears (on offense) in the middle of the season."

I believe it because his motor never stops. Today, he's as passionate about what he does for a living as he was the December 1983 day Colonel John Clune, the late, great AFA athletic director, promoted him to replace Ken Hatfield, who returned home to coach Arkansas.

I believe it because in September 1997, with his Falcons that Saturday having just scored a 24-0 nationally televised knockout of rival Colorado State en route to a 7-0 start, Fisher called me at home at 3:15 the next morning. A voter in the

USA Today/ESPN Coaches top 25 poll, he wanted to know if I had some West Coast scores from the previous night's games. He was working on his top 25 for that week's poll.

A groggy Burrows: "Uh, hello?"

A wide-awake DeBerry: "Mike? Fisher DeBerry. I hope I'm not bothering you."

Burrows: "Uh, no, coach, you're not."

DeBerry: "Well, I missed some scores on TV and I figured if anybody had them, you would."

Burrows: "Uh, scores? You need scores?"

DeBerry: "Yeah, how'd UCLA do?"

Burrows: "Uh, they won."

DeBerry: "That's what I needed to know. Thank you, and have a good day."

Most coaches who "vote" in the USA Today/ESPN top 25 poll have their sports information directors compile and cast the ballot. The reason? Most coaches believe they're too busy to spare the time. Sleepily, I learned Fisher isn't one of them.

I believe it because of what Fisher believes in.

Faith, family and the Falcons.

Forever.

A devout Christian. Devoted husband, father and now, grandfather. A coach and man with few peers.

A few years ago, recovering from colon surgery in a Denver hospital, the first telephone call I received was from Fisher. "Down here at the Academy," he said, "we're all thinking of you."

He was beaming, understandably, after Dallas Thompson's nationally televised overtime field goal at Notre Dame Stadium in October 1996 gave the Falcons a shocking 20-17 victory over the heavily favored Irish.

Yet the proudest, if not happiest, I remember Air Force's

coach being in a sports setting was when he watched his son, Joe, play for Clemson in the College World Series.

Air Force hit a home run 20 years ago when it brought Fisher DeBerry, his wife, Lu Ann, and their family to the Academy.